Charles
Redd
Monographs
in Western
History No. 13

After 150 Years

The Latter-day Saints in Sesquicentennial Perspective

Thomas G. Alexander
and
Jessie L. Embry

Editors

Charles Redd Center for Western Studies

*The Charles Redd Monographs in Western
History are made possible by a grant from
Charles Redd. This grant served as the basis
for the establishment of the Charles Redd
Center for Western Studies at Brigham Young
University.*

*Center editors: Thomas G. Alexander
Howard A. Christy*

ISBN   0-941214-08-7

Charles Redd Center for Western Studies
© 1983 by Charles Redd Center for Western Studies.
All rights reserved.
Printed in the United States of America

Distributed by Signature Books, Midvale, Utah

Contents

Introduction
Thomas G. Alexander vii

1 In the Presence of the Past:
Continuity and Change in
Twentieth-Century Mormonism
Jan Shipps 1

2 A Demographic Portrait of
the Mormons, 1830-1980
Dean L. May 37

3 For the Strength of the Hills:
Imagining Mormon Country
Edward A. Geary 71

4 The Dawning of a Brighter Day:
Mormon Literature After 150 Years
Eugene England 95

5 The Church Moves Outside the
United States: Some Observations
from South America
F. LaMond Tullis 147

6 Testimony and Technology:
A Phase of the Modernization
of Mormonism since 1950
James B. Allen 171

Introduction

Thomas G. Alexander

During 1980, the sesquicentennial year of the Church of Jesus Christ of Latter-day Saints, members reviewed, reconsidered, and celebrated their past. A special session of the Church's April annual conference originated from the Whitmer home in Fayette, New York, where the Church was organized 150 years before. Commemorative and reflective events ranging from dances to symposia were held throughout the Church. Church members were called upon to remember their traditions and to rededicate themselves to spreading the gospel throughout the world.

As part of the sesquicentennial observance, the directors of the Charles Redd Center for Western Studies asked a group of scholars to reexamine certain aspects of the Church's development over the past century and a half. The results of that reexamination are presented here in essay form.

If these essays have one common theme, it is that of adaptation to change. In the lead essay, Jan Shipps reinterprets the implications of the changes that took place during the acculturation of the Latter-day Saints in the late nineteenth and early twentieth centuries. Her central theme is the process by which the Latter-day Saints moved from living in mythic time to living in a world that allowed them to recreate the times of the beginning in their own lives and experiences.

In the second essay, Dean May examines the demographic profile of the Latter-day Saints, principally in the nineteenth century. His data allows us to review much that we had already known or suspected and to understand much that had not been previously understood, such as the suprisingly large 40 percent of the Church membership that did not go west from Nauvoo, and the high-percentage of immigrant population of nineteenth-century Mormon communities in Utah.

The next two essays consider imaginative works about the Mormons. Edward Geary examines the popular images centering around the village that separated the Latter-day Saint people from other nineteenth-century frontier types. Eugene England, in a survey of Mormon literature, argues that after a long period of less-than-distinguished literature the Latter-day Saint community is now producing a group of authors who are writing works of lasting literary significance.

The last two essays consider two of the most important contemporary indications of change. LaMond Tullis looks at the expansion of the Church into Latin America, and in doing so he recognizes the successes and challenges accompanying the unprecedented growth within a culture quite unlike the Anglo-American traditions of the United States. James Allen, in the concluding essay, examines the impact of technological changes as leaders have adapted computer technology, standardized building design, and microfilm to the needs of Church programs.

1

In the Presence of the Past: Continuity and Change in Twentieth-Century Mormonism

Jan Shipps

A difficult problem for students of the Latter-day Saint experience has been to understand the meaning of the changes from nineteenth- to twentieth-century Mormonism. As Jan Shipps, Associate Professor of History and Religious Studies and Director of the Center for American Studies at Indiana University-Purdue University at Indianapolis, points out in the following essay, arguments have ranged all the way from the explanation that the change involved nothing of significance to the position that everything worthwhile was lost.

By applying the methodology of the history of religions to the problem and using the comparative approach, Professor Shipps has produced an important and heuristically useful paper. She argues that there were changes—significant changes—and that they can best be understood by examining the world view that each condition represented. From a new religious tradition in which the members were personally immersed in the creation and maintenance of a new world in the nineteenth century, the Mormons have become a church in which each member defines his or her relationship to other communicants and to those outside the fold by adherence to a particular code of conduct. No longer do Mormon leaders and members expect to separate themselves physically from the gentiles of the world. The separation in now psychic.

Shipps also argues that the tendency to see Mormonism as another Protestant sect is not only mistaken but misleading since the basis of many Latter-day Saint beliefs that seem to bear a resemblance to those of evangelical Protestants is quite different. She sees particularly the ideas of chosenness and of millennialism as important examples.

If a group of modern Latter-day Saints—say a dozen or so drawn from the 170,547 members of the Church who were added to the rolls in 1976—should be transported by means of a magical time machine back to 1880, they would find the world of Mormondom a century ago very unfamiliar territory. In addition to a landscape from which is missing a multiplicity of ward chapels all built according to standardized architectural plans, and besides all the obvious differences between a Mormonism that had its being in a more technologically primitive world than this one, such a hypothetical Latter-day Saint (LDS) group would suddenly come face to face with the reality of plural marriage. Rather than knowing about the nineteenth-century form of the patriarchal order of marriage only in abstract terms, they would meet polygamy head on. But these things that are so clearly a part of a different age might not make the Mormonism of 1880 seem as unfamiliar to modern Mormons as would a host of other, far more subtle, differences.

If these Saints, by chance, stepped from their time machine out into the land of Zion on the morning of the first Sunday of the month, they would find families unabashedly eating hearty breakfasts. Disoriented as much by the discovery that the day was not being treated as a day of fasting as by "time-machine lag," the latter-day visitors would most probably seek out a ward meeting place, believing that they could get their bearings by attending Sunday School. Instead of finding what would seem normal to them, a neatly departmentalized session organized by age groups, they would find a somewhat motley general assembly of children of mixed ages. Staying to observe what was happening, they would be reassured by the familiar "faith-promoting" gist of the words. Yet, accustomed to the interesting approach and varied activities of twentieth-century Sunday School situations, they would be surprised and, perhaps, impatient with what would appear to them as interminable "reading around" from the pages of the *Juvenile Instructor*.

Expecting to be able to attend sacrament meeting in the same local ward immediately after Sunday School, the visitors would learn that sacrament meeting was only held in the tabernacle located in the center of town. This would cause them to expect to join with all the Saints in the area in a large-scale worship service, but that would likewise lead to disappointment since at the appointed hour the tabernacle would still seem virtually empty. In time, disorientation would give way to dismay: a brother with a "tobacco habit" could well be seated on the stand; another brother's shirt might be so marked with coffee stains that the visitors would certainly know he indulged in that forbidden beverage; from still another, conceivably a bishop's counselor, might be wafting from the stand across the front rows in the building the telltale aroma of a recently consumed toddy. Yet despite their shock at such open breaches of the Word of Wisdom, the members of this latter-day group would almost certainly be equally astonished to see that the meeting proceeded toward its conclusion without any circulating head-counter collecting quantifiable data that would allow the brethren in Salt Lake City to measure the Saints' level of active commitment to Mormonism.

Moreover, modern Mormons are accustomed to participating in flawlessly orchestrated conference sessions via television. Had these interlopers from the future dropped in at conference time instead of visiting on an ordinary Sunday, the disorientation level would surely reach the crisis stage. It is very possible that upon hearing one of the many variations on John Henry Smith's opening statement in his 1885 annual conference address "What the Lord may have for me to say to you I cannot imagine", the visitors would simply leave, fleeing forward to their familiar twentieth-century Mormon world as fast as their time machine could carry them.

Wondering about the discrepancy between what they had seen on the one hand and their lovingly nurtured faith-promoting picture of Mormonism's pioneer past on the other, these hypothetical Saints would no doubt worry about how they ought to describe their experience in forthcoming talks at sacrament meeting. Some members of the group would probably decide to talk about the inspiring beauty of the Great Salt Lake Valley. Others would perhaps emphasize the timelessness of the *Juvenile Instructor* story the Sunday School youngsters had been stumbling through. But quite possibly one among the dozen would find an occasion to present a really honest, straightforward report of the trip. And if that should happen, in all likelihood the result would be an inadvertent, but nevertheless serious, misrepresentation of the nineteenth-century Mormon past.

This perplexing riddle of how a truly and totally honest report of the nineteenth-century LDS experience could convey a false impression of the Mormon pioneer past is baffling and worrisome. But it also can have heuristic value since a consideration of this enigma, this perplexing situation, lays bare an enormous problem that historians who deal with religious movements have had to face ever since the Rankean notion that the goal of history is reporting things "as they actually were" was married to scientific history with its appetite for cold, hard, unassailable fact.

When religion is the subject matter, the sacred is as important as the not-sacred. But since the sacred and the not-sacred are simply "different modes of being in the world," empirical evidence does not always discriminate between them.[1] Therefore, historians who have attempted to abide by the canons of historical scholarship, while at the same time attempting to reconstruct the past history of religious movements, have developed a two-step procedure that makes getting around this difficulty possible. They (and I am one of them) use belief statements, descriptions of worship activity, documented—and thus demonstrable—compliance with religious rituals, and acceptance of clearly articulated ethical systems to demonstrate that the reality of the sacred was accepted by the participants in the historical drama. With that established, they move on to explicate the historical situation, treating the sacred and profane (as Mircea Eliade denotes the not-sacred) with essentially the same set of narrative and analytic tools.

As long as a religious movement is institutionalized or developed so fully that a more or less direct relationship exists between manifestations of the sacred and certain empirically identifiable religious statements and activities, this approach works very well. Indeed, it works so well that it may be described as the "orthodox" scholarly approach to religious history. But this approach is less useful when religious movements are either (a) coming into existence or (b) undergoing radical change. At such crucial times in the history of religious movements, the sacred and the not-sacred cannot always be clearly delineated and separated out. Belief statements are often ambiguous and more than ordinarily subject to multiple interpretation; worship activity cannot always be identified as worship activity; rituals are poorly developed or nonexistent, and so on.

As the foregoing suggests, that honest hypothetical Saint's straightforward account of his nineteenth-century visit to Zion would misrepresent the reality of the LDS pioneer experience because *in illo tempore*, "in those times," things are not always what they seem. For this reason, if the "orthodox" scholarly approach is used in writing the history of such periods, the result sometimes poses such a "myth versus reality" problem that an alternative approach is required. That this is the case is not a new observation. The recognition of the need for an alternative approach to the history of religions that are coming into being or undergoing radical change stands at the base not only of the important "Social World of Early Christianity" movement in New Testament studies, but of a comparable

"Social World of Ancient Israel" movement in Old Testament studies.[2] These two movements are, in turn, based on the literature of theoretical anthropology, a literature that is filled with an ever-increasing number of studies of religions either coming into being or undergoing radical change.

The specific problem being confronted in this essay is continuity and change in Mormonism. This calls for some treatment of the *before* as well as the *after*. But since Mormonism was still coming into being during the last half of the nineteenth century, an alternative approach to the earlier time period will be used. Rather, however, than drawing directly on anthropoligical literature to clarify what was happening during the pioneer period, as Lawrence Foster has done with such great success in his study of plural marriage, or making use of the same set of categories that anthropologist Mark P. Leone used in comparing the pioneer and modern periods in *The Roots of Modern Mormonism*, the alternative to the standard orthodox approach to the history of nineteenth-century Utah Mormonism to be employed here is an approach drawn from the discipline with the somewhat misleading name: *history of religions*.[3] Because it is concerned as much with phenomenological and structural questions as with historical ones, this approach lends itself to the explications of situations when things are not always what they appear to be on the surface. Using it will make possible the identification of the major points of difference between the Mormonism of the pioneer era and that of the modern age.

A catalog of items—some of enormous significance and others only trivial but interesting—could be developed to detail the difference between nineteenth- and twentieth-century Mormonism. Yet, as fascinating as such a mere listing could be, it is not a necessary prologue to this consideration of continuity and change, for there is general agreement that, at least superficially, the difference between the two is very great indeed. More particularly, scholarly consensus extends to the notion that not only is pioneer Mormonism different from modern Mormonism, but that external pressure (especially political pressure from the United States government) played such an enormous role in forcing the Mormons to change that it is simply impossible to make sense out of LDS pioneer history without taking that pressure into account.[4] (This outside pressure took many forms, but it became concentrated in an antipolygamy campaign of intense virulence in the 1880s.) Virtually universal agreement exists, too, that buried within that antipolygamy campaign were issues as much economic and political as social and moral. Scholars pretty well agree also that although it could have been initiated as *assimilative* reform (that is, reform activity through which culturally dominant reformers offer their less-fortunate neighbors the possibility of adopting the reformers' life patterns and, thus, the possibility of achieving middle-class respectability), the antipolygamy campaign came to be almost exclusively *coercive* reform as time went on. Just as prohibition would become coercive when temperance leaders started to see persons who drank as "intractable defenders of another culture," (that is, persons who rejected the reformers' values and did not want to change), so antipolygamy became a coercive movement when it became obvious—remember the abortive effort to establish a refuge for polygamous wives, for example—that the practice of plural marriage was not forced on the community by its religious leaders.[5] Finally, scholarly consensus points to LDS Church President Wilford Woodruff's 1890 announcement that the Mormon Church had stopped performing plural marriage as the effective point of division between the past and the present. Beyond that, consensus disintegrates, however.

There is no question that from a doctrinal standpoint, President Woodruff's Manifesto (as the document containing his announcement is called) has comparable status with the revelations found in the Doctrine and Covenants of the Church of Jesus Christ of Latter-day Saints. But since the evidence is ambiguous—depending on an interpretation of a diary entry in which Woodruff noted that he had concluded after an intense period of prayer and contemplation that he must act for the "temporal salvation" of the Church—scholarly opinion, and popular opinion too, divides on the matter of motivation, on what it was that led President Woodruff to reverse his position on the patriarchal order of marriage.[6] Disagreement also exists about the real intent of Woodruff's announcement since evidence about that is even more ambiguous. Because the historical record includes a good deal of evidence that suggests the Manifesto was actually a temporary expedient designed to relieve external pressure long enough for Utah to gain entrance to the Union, it is not at all certain the Manifesto was an announcement that the practice of plural marriage would not be part of Mormonism from the point of its issue forward.[7] But there is no way to know for certain whether the Mormon president-prophet's intention was directing the Saints to eschew polygamy permanently. The elections of Brigham H. Roberts to the U.S. House of Representatives and Reed Smoot to the U.S. Senate came so closely on the heels of Utah's acquisition of statehood that the hands of the antipolygamists were forced. They had no choice; they had to see that Woodruff's announcement was treated as a substantive pledge to bring the practice of polygamy to an end. Since we can never know whether, as in the case of prohibition, a *gesture* indicating symbolic capitulation to the ascendancy of the evangelical Protestant culture would have sufficed, it is only possible to speculate about whether gradual reinstitution of plural marriage could have been effected in much the same manner that the gradual reintroduction of the consumption of alcoholic beverages was effected and eventually gained widespread acceptance.[8] In any case, though speculation about this matter is interesting, it opens more windows onto American social change and the political processes that develop in pluralistic cultures than onto Mormonism.

Whatever President Woodruff's motivation or intent in issuing the Manifesto, plural marriage has not been reintroduced into Mormonism except among splinter groups. The Manifesto signalled the beginning of the end of a Mormon world in which plural marriage was not only tolerated, but celebrated. But it did more than that. Because it was a part of an unstated bargain that on one side involved a fundamental alteration in the manner of the exercise of Mormon political and economic power as well as the discontinuation of plural marriage, and on the other side made possible the institutional survival of the Church of Jesus Christ of Latter-day Saints as well as the entrance of the Mormon state into the federal union, the Manifesto was an announcement that the old order would have to pass away. As important as are all the practical questions, such as the extent to which external pressure caused this to happen when and as it did, and the manner in which a new *modus vivendi* was fashioned that made possible the secure establishment of the new Mormon order within the context of American society and culture, the question of concern here is what happened to Mormonism when the old order passed away.

Having removed themselves to the Great Basin, the nineteenth-century Saints tried to stay unspotted from the world by as far as possible separating themselves politically, economically, socially, and psychically from the rest of humanity. When the Manifesto symbolically set aside the boundaries that had been so painfully constructed and maintained, a period of extreme danger commenced. At stake was the sheer survival not of the LDS Church itself, but of a Mormonism that continued to preserve its exclusive claim to be the sole corporate body in possession of the holy priesthood and invested with the status of God's chosen people. Without boundaries to set them apart, without "gentiles" to stand over and against, a chosen people cannot exist; their very identity depends on their perception of specialness; and that specialness, in turn, depends on their being separated in some way from that part of the population that is not special. The United States government had made it clear that institutionally established and maintained boundaries could not be tolerated in this nation, and this meant the Latter-day Saints were faced with a serious internal problem. Somehow the responsibility for boundary maintenance had to be shifted from the corporate body to the individuals within that body, and that shift had to be legitimated in such a way that it would gain general acceptance.

This was no small task, nor one that could be accomplished quickly or easily, especially as it had to be carried out under the watchful eye of the *Salt Lake Tribune* (a hostile gentile newspaper), the Utah Republican Party, the United States government, and the nation's evangelical Christian community. The Saints had to have time to learn that, instead of leaving the separation of Mormons and gentiles primarily up to the Church leadership, they must develop individual patterns of behavior with which they could keep themselves unspotted from the world. A period of transition was inevitable, and this period lasted a very long time, possibly all the way through the ecclesiastical administrations of Presidents Joseph F. Smith and Heber J. Grant. But notwithstanding the time it took, the heretofore corporate responsibility for maintaining LDS identity that had been assumed by the central church leadership was transferred to the general membership.

This transfer of responsibility to the individual was so successful that it brought about a profound alteration in Mormonism. The change proved in time to be so basic that some interpreters have suggested that, in its new emphasis on individual behavior, Mormonism had turned into a proto-Protestant movement. When this interpretation is set out with great sophistication, as it is in Klaus Hansen's

Mormonism and the American Experience, the interpretation has a good deal of explanatory power.[9] But when such an interpretation is superficially stated and then used—by suggesting that Mormonism is an idiosyncratic Protestant denomination, charging the Latter-day Saints with whole-sale acceptance of the Protestant ethic, and treating these allegations as proved—to explain the fabled wealth of the Saints and their church, it confuses rather than clarifies the picture.[10]

Still another interpretation that draws on the shifting of responsibility to individual Saints is the one around which Mark Leone builds the basic argument of his *Roots of Modern Mormonism*. Commenting on what happened following the issuing of the Manifesto, he described the disappearance of political and economic centralization, but differing from Hansen who suggests in his "Epilogue" to *Quest for Empire* that the political kingdom gave way to a powerful, centralized Mormon Church, Leone sees a switch from Mormon state to a Mormon Church that is theologically diffuse. The switch Leone sees is not a transfer of responsibility for boundary maintenance, but a delegation to individual Saints of the task of constructing their own personal versions of the way in which Mormons ought to view the world; that is, of developing their own individual understandings of the Mormon world view.[11]

Many additional suggestions about what happened to Mormonism during the transition period that followed the Manifesto are to be found in the literature. In *The Story of the Latter-day Saints*, for instance, James B. Allen and Glen M. Leonard picture the two or three decades following 1890 as a time of "inspired accommodation," while in *The Mormon Experience*, Leonard J. Arrington and Davis Bitton describe the "creative adjustment" that took place within Mormonism during those years. [12]

In addition to the explanations found in recent substantive and important surveys that more or less treat the whole of the Mormon past, there are oversimplified explanations that range all the way from "The Manifesto Was a Victory!"—Gordon Thomasson's rosy characterization wherein the Latter-day Saints (he makes no distinction between the Church and its members) hold on to everything that really mattered—to Samuel W. Taylor's entertaining yet rueful account of a post-Manifesto period in which everything of real value in Mormonism is tragically and irretrievably lost.[13] The fundamental way in which the various historical accounts differ provides a dramatic illustration of how very difficult it is to find out from the secondary literature what really happened during these critical years of transition.

Although working directly with the sources can clarify things to some extent, the very fact that the transition period lends itself to such a multiplicity of treatments is an important indication that the period was marked by so much ambiguity and confusion that the documents themselves provide no clear picture of exactly what happened. Since the passage of time rather than contemporary opinions about what was going on determined the way in which Mormonism would develop, the historical record reveals less about the way in which Mormonism did and did not change during the transition period than about the context in which change or lack of change occurred. A better picture of what happened can be delineated if a comparison is made between pioneer Mormonism and the Mormonism of the modern age.

The Church of Jesus Christ of Latter-day Saints came into being in 1830. During its first fourteen years it was led by Joseph Smith, the prophet who at the age of 24 had published the Book of Mormon, a work he claimed to have translated from metal plates unearthed, at the direction of an angel, from a hill in western New York. Considered by the Saints as scripture, this book was cast in the form of a historical narrative covering a thousand years of pre-Columbian history; it featured the story of the adventures, vicissitudes, and final extinction of a Hebraic family that traveled by sailing ship to the western hemisphere, as well as an account of a visit Christ made to the New World at the end of his mortal life. In addition to the Book of Mormon that identified America as the promised land and latter-day revelation that told them they were living in the new and everlasting dispensation of the fulness of times, the Latter-day Saints believed also that the Old Testament orders of Aaron and Melchizedek had been restored to the earth and that members of these priesthoods presided over them.

Taken altogether, along with the surety that their prophet was blessed with the gift of continuing revelation, these beliefs transformed those who repented and were baptized into the Church from ordinary American farmers and craftsmen into God's elect, his chosen people. Yet, while theirs was an exclusive claim based on the position that when God executed a new and perpetual covenant with them in 1830 all existing covenants were null and void, the Saints were not the only Americans who believed themselves to be the chosen people. Among others, there were Presbyterians, Baptists, Quakers, and even Methodists who regarded themselves as legitimate heirs to God's promises and, thus, as his chosen as well. But the difference between what that claim meant to the great body of evangelical Protestants, who dominated the American religious scene in the first half of the nineteenth century, and what it meant to the Latter-day Saints is extremely instructive. The evangelical conception of being chosen differed from the conception of being chosen that underlay and supported the Latter-day Saints. For the evangelical Protestant the claim was a scripturally based doctrinal assumption that had to be brought to life through an experiential assurance of salvation given to individuals by Jesus Christ. The initiative that accorded chosen status came from outside man. A conscious desire to be a part of the elect demonstrated by repentance and a request for baptism into the Church that was the corporate body of God's people was not enough. Perhaps for that reason the experience of salvation—of being saved—became, in time, more important to evangelicals than the doctrine of election. For Latter-day Saints, on the other hand, the claim to chosenness was not a contingent claim. The power of the LDS message rested to a great degree on the condition that the "field was white to the harvest." Through faith, repentance, baptism, and confirmation into the Church of Jesus Christ, individuals gained entrance into the chosen community; they became citizens of God's elect nation, newly restored to the earth. For nineteenth-century evangelical Protestants, then, being a part of the chosen people was a theological construct that had less immediacy than the salvation experience, while for the Latter-day Saints, after a revelation called for the "gathering" of the Saints and after the building of the Kirtland Temple, the claim to chosenness became the principle around which they ordered their existence. For the evangelicals chosenness was symbolic; for the Mormons it was literal.[14]

Although this elevation to primacy of the notion that their identity as God's chosen people has been more fundamental to the Latter-day Saint experience than anything else might seem to challenge the work of the many scholars who have pointed to the kingdom of God as the controlling metaphor of early Mormonism, it is not so meant. Rather it is intended to underscore the importance of the kingdom of God from another quarter. One key to understanding the differences between the LDS version and other Christian primitivist versions of the gospel is noting the crucial difference in their restoration claims. While others preached that the New Testament apostolic church was restored and ready to accept new communicants, the Latter-day Saints spread the "good news" of the beginning of the literal gathering of Israel and the restoration of the ten tribes, as well as the organization of a church that was led by a prophet and God's holy priesthood, also restored to the earth in these latter days. Organized with apostles, prophets, pastors, teachers, evangelists, and so on, this Church of Jesus Christ claimed to have in its sole possession the gospel ordinances and authority by which individuals willing to repent and be baptized could be *adopted into Israel* in the Old Testament meaning of the term.[15] As converts responded to this powerful message, the body of God's people grew, and since the kingdom of God is the abode of God's people, its reestablishment on the earth followed, as the night the day, the gathering, the promise of restoration of the ten tribes of Israel, and the restoration of the priesthoods of Aaron and Melchizedek. Notwithstanding the imprecision about whether the literal kingdom of God was already or was just about to be rebuilt that is found in LDS literature from the beginning—an imprecision, interestingly enough, that has a parallel in the Pauline letters in the New Testament—the LDS missionary message carries within it an implicit promise of a life lived out in God's kingdom.[16] As John Henry Smith (in that address with the "What the Lord may have for me to say to you I cannot imagine" opening) reported to general conference about the missionary effort in England, "We have done the best we could in our ministrations among the people, and have striven with the power that the Lord has given us to warn our fellowmen of the reestablishment of the kingdom of God," so thousands of LDS missionaries before and since have carried the message of the reestablishment of the kingdom of God, not in the future, but in the present.[17]

While it may be that the realization that they were citizens of an elect nation came to the Saints only with the beginning of the gathering of Israel and construction of the Kirtland Temple, it is important to understand, particularly in the context of history-of-religions theory, that the designation of the Latter-day Saints as the chosen people in the United States in the early 1830s had the same ontological significance for Mormons as God's designating as chosen the descendants of Abraham. In each situation the appropriate response to powerfully perceived manifestations of the sacred was the building up of a separated community, one clearly set apart so that distinctions were easy to make between the chosen people and the not-chosen gentiles. Moreover, in that act of building up such a community, the Saints were, from a phenomenological standpoint, participating in a paradigmatic act of creation. The apocalyptic fervor that pervaded early LDS thought was a natural expression, then, of the desire that an act of creating awakens in man "to live," as Mircea Eliade puts it, "in a pure and holy cosmos as it was in the beginning, when it came fresh from the Creator's hands."[18]

But to oversimplify, as in the matter of differences between evangelical Christianity's conception of the restoration of the apostolic church and the Latter-day Saints' conception of the literal gathering of Israel and the restoration of the ten tribes, so evangelical Christian millennial thought tended to look for inspiration to the New Testament book of Revelation while the Saints looked both to the New Testament and backward to what one Old Testament scholar describes as the *Dawn of Apocalyptic*, the Old Testament prophets and, most especially, the Book of Daniel.[19] Therefore, while the evangelical Christians watched for a holy city descending out of heaven at the end of time, the Latter-day Saints set about building a counterpart of the Hebraic kingdom with Solomon's Temple at its center, developing at the same time a literal latter-day counterpart of their conception of the Old Testament Hebraic culture.[20]

Accounts of the consequences of this effort—internal strife and external pressure eventuating in the murder of the Mormon prophet and the destruction of Nauvoo, the LDS kingdom on the Mississippi—are so familiar that summary is not a necessary prologue to a consideration of the importance of the concepts of the kingdom of God, being chosen as the elect, the promised land, and Zion in the Mormon pioneer experience. The fact that Mormonism was rent at least in twain before the Saints crossed the Mississippi is so significant, however, that the implications of that break deserve a brief consideration.

From the beginning the Mormon movement had held in suspension conceptions of the LDS gospel that were fundamentally contradictory. On the one hand there were Saints who understood the Mormon message and accepted its substance metaphorically, and on the other there were Saints who accepted the gospel quite literally. Although apostasy was a common phenomenon in the early years, the discrepancy between these two understandings did not make itself fully known until Joseph Smith's death removed from the Mormon community the intellect (and the spiritual nature, if you will) that was the medium within which these elements had been suspended. After 1844 the two elements started to separate out, and by 1847, when the Saints started west under the leadership of Brigham Young, those whose understanding of the Mormon message was mainly metaphysical generally stayed behind.[21] As a result, the Saints who crossed the plains and climbed the mountains to reach the Great Basin were preternaturally disposed to conceive of their trek as a repetition of the journey of the Israelites through the wilderness to the promised land.

The parallels between the Mormon trek and the Exodus and between Brigham Young and Moses have been so often pointed out that their very mention seems almost a cliché. Yet to neglect the parallel is to misconstrue the pioneer experience, for just as the original designation of the Saints as chosen was a repetition of God's paradigmatic act in choosing Abraham's seed, so the Mormon trek renewed the force of God's election of the Mormons in precisely the same way that the miraculous departure from Egypt and the journey through the wilderness and into the promised land renewed the identity of the Hebraic tribes as the citizens of His elect nation. Moreover, the full symbolic import of the Mormon trek is barely perceptible without the realization that despite the conscious drawing of parallels—division into tens and fifties with captains over them and so on—this was no ritual recreation of a sacred event celebrated for purposes of remembering God's mercy to his people. When Brigham Young led the Saints across the plains, he led them not only out of the hands of their midwestern persecutors, but backward into a primordial sacred time. As the original Israelites had been, so these new Israelites were "once again at the beginning," *in illo tempore*. Repeating the passage from chaos to cosmos, the Latter-day Saints, by that very passage out of a place confused by a concatenation of religious claims into one where their calling and election were unquestionably sure, were formed not into a culture whose perpetuation depended on the preservation of a particular *polis*, but into an ethnic body, a chosen race.[22] Once they had been no people; now, in truth, they were God's people, but not so much because, "like living stones" they had built themselves "into a spiritual house to be a holy priesthood." Like the children of Israel, the Saints made their way through the wilderness to claim their "inheritances," and in so doing conjoined experience and scripture to take possession of that special relationship to God that once had been the sole property of the Jews.[23]

In explicating the dichotomy between mythic (sacred) time and linear, historical (not-sacred, profane) time, Guilford Dudley III, in a very useful study, *Religion on Trial*, states that "the mythic time of beginnings is sacred by definition."[24] The task the Mormons confronted in the Great Basin was nothing less than starting at the beginning to people a holy land and build God's kingdom. If Dudley is right, the entry of Brigham Young and his followers into the Great Salt Lake Valley was not only entry into sacred space—that is, into the promised land—but a move that carried them even more deeply into sacred time. But is there any indication that he is right? After all, nineteenth-century Latter-day Saints were practical people, equally able to benefit from trade with gentiles who crossed their territory on the way to the California gold fields as to build tabernacles and temples in which to glorify God. Did the Saints know that they were living outside time? Since the surviving documents can hardly be expected to yield a *direct* answer to this question, is there any way to find out?

Perhaps an analogue drawn from the experience of a different chosen people will be useful. Richard Rubenstein, a rabbi turned scholar, essayist, and college professor, visited Israel soon after the United Nations certified its existence as a sovereign state. *Power Struggle*, Rubenstein's autobiography, includes an account of that visit and his reaction to it.[25] Then, among the essays collected in *After Auschwitz: Radical Theology and Contemporary Judaism* is one that deals with "The Rebirth of Israel in Contemporary Jewish Theology." This essay is a more impersonal and intellectual consideration of the situation, but it clearly reflects the fact that Rubenstein was in Israel in those heady days when Israel, the political state, and Zion, the symbolic Hebraic kingdom, were fused in Israeli minds. Such great expectations of an impending entrance into the millennium prevailed that they produced an attitude whose "most characteristic feature [was] its fervid desire to bring time and history to an ending."[26] The tenuous and dangerous position of the new Jewish homeland in the volatile Middle Eastern political cauldron appeared to matter less to the Zionists than their need to make history come full circle, allowing them to be again in the original Israel. While news of the events of the world was freely available, people paid attention to their own concerns, taking little thought for the morrow or for what was going on outside Zion.[27] Whether the analogy is appropriate is, perhaps, less important than the fact that it directs attention to the way in which messianic and millennial movements lift otherwise everyday practical people out of time by making long-range plans untenable in view of the nearness of the eschaton. Since ample evidence indicates that the Mormon pioneers were prepared for the winding-up scene to commence at an early date, and since expectations of the end divert attention away from the calendar and the clock, history and theory here converge.

Although the nineteenth-century Latter-day Saints may have stood outside time as a consequence of their expectations of the advent of the millennium, this does not mean that what they built was insubstantial and other-worldly. On the contrary, they built what was, in effect, a nation-state that was internally powerful and externally respected as strong enough to be dangerous, even dangerous to the United States government itself. Gentile politicians maintained tenuous control over its territorial government, but if anyone's word was law in Utah, née Deseret, it was the president of the LDS Church. Surely Mark Leone overstates the extent of the independence of the Mormon state during the pioneer era, but he is nevertheless correct when he says that in many ways this was Mormonism's golden age.[28] Before the Saints were placed under siege in the 1880s, their nation-state was reasonably independent economically and socially.[29] It had its own diplomatic department; and although its political strength has probably been considerably exaggerated, at least it had its own independent political organization in the shadow government of the State of Deseret.[30]

But if outstanding individual effort and extraordinary community accomplishment together built cities, towns, tabernacles and temples, railroads, factories, stores, industries, and all the paraphernalia of a surprisingly strong and independent literal kingdom, what of the Mormon religious experience therein? While there is always danger in analogy and the development of generalization therefrom, Rabbi Rubenstein's observations about the initial Israeli Zionic experience can be helpful at this point. As an American rabbi, he was concerned and disappointed at seeing an almost total absence of ritualized worship in Israel until it occurred to him that persons living in the kingdom need not observe rituals that are reminders of what it once was like to live in the kingdom. Realizing that more than anything else a good part of Jewish ritual seemed designed as a reminder of what "next year in Jerusalem" would be like, he looked about not for ordinary worship forms, but for expressive ways of celebrating being, as it were, in Jerusalem, and found that most intensively expressed in Israeli folk music.[31]

Much ink in Mormon historiography has been spread across many history pages to develop the importance of the millennial idea. But when the excellent *Building the City of God* study or almost any volume of the *Journal of Discourses* is read with a sensitive ear for the language, it is plain to see and hear that John Henry Smith's placing of the reestablishment of the kingdom of God in the present tense was not a slip of the tongue.[32] While Christ had not come to earth to reign, nineteenth-century Saints nevertheless lived so clearly "in the kingdom" *in illo tempore*, that the sacred and not-sacred simply cannot be considered separately. This is not to say that dancing rather than formal worship was the order of the period, for in addition to singing and dancing there were places of worship in every town, and worship services were held in them. Still, as it was for the Jews who emigrated to Israel soon after the Second World War, the essential worship in the LDS pioneer world was building up the kingdom and inhabiting it.[33] The hypothetical Saints returning from the twentieth century in a time machine would have been astonished to find so few Saints at sacrament meeting because in the twentieth century sacrament meeting is a visible worship sign, whereas in the pioneer era more expressive worship signs were irrigation canals or neatly built and nicely decorated houses or good crops of sugar beets.[34] More significant, living in the kingdom in the nineteenth century was the sign of citizenship in God's elect nation. Gentiles there were, but the community was a separated one, made special through the institution of the patriarchal order of marriage. While the Word of Wisdom was usually observed in the Mormon community, the Latter-day Saint perception of being special, of being a part of the chosen people, did not depend on abstaining from tobacco and coffee and universally negative decisions about whether or not to drink the Valley Tan or the wine the Saints manufactured in Dixie.[35] Identity was maintained corporately, not individually, which explains why all the citizens of the kingdom—those who were involved in plural marriage and those who were not—were willing to defend to the last possible moment the practice of polygamy that kept them set apart.[36]

No single explanation ever suffices to explain complex historical events, and the Manifesto is no exception. Many factors entered into the development of the overall context within which President Woodruff had to take the problem of what to do to the Lord in that intense session of prayer he described in his diary entry for 25 September 1890.[37] It is possible, however, to observe that when the Manifesto signalled the end of plural marriage, it also signalled the beginning of the end of the extraordinary situation wherein Latter-day Saints had lived their lives in sacred space and sacred time. They had expected the parousia; instead they were ushered into a profane environment.

Evidence of many different kinds may be used to demonstrate that the 1890 Manifesto was a disconfirming event that profoundly altered the character of Mormonism. For example, the development of a fundamentalist movement that has as its implicit purpose the recreation of the nineteenth-century Mormon experience is, ipso facto, an indication that Mormonism has been radically changed.[38] Another somewhat paradoxical indication of the impact on the Mormon community and of changes the Manifesto implied is a subsequent growth spurt in the turn-of-the-century decades.

In a conceptually useful study of a modern prophetic movement, Leon Festinger and others hypothesize that disconfirmation leads to increased rather than decreased missionary activity as a group that has experienced a disconfirming event seeks to bolster its beliefs through convincing others of their truth.[39] Unless an abnormal birthrate accounts for a temporary rise in natural membership increase in the LDS Church, the fact that the steady growth rate of around 2.6 percent that obtained with surprising consistency in the decades of the 1880s, 1890s, 1920s, 1930s, and 1940s increased in the turn-of-the-century decade to 3.9 percent and stayed above 3 percent in the following ten-year period is statistically significant, and at least superficially confirms the Festinger hypothesis.[40]

But such indirect evidence is not needed to substantiate the notion that in the years following the Manifesto the Saints had a disconfirmation situation to deal with. Even though, as indicated earlier, the transition years have been much written about without any consensus emerging as to what was really going on, the historical literature reveals that the cessation of plural marriage was such a disconfirming event that it thrust the Saints into the modern age. Interpreted in a phenomenological context, the very ambiguity of the historical accounts reflects an ambiguity that infects society as the natural and inevitable consequence of passage out of sacred time into profane, linear, historical time.

The study of early Christianity provides a useful parallel to this aspect of the Mormon past. At this point in their history the Saints had to face a situation somewhat similar to the one that faced the early Christians in the late first century when the synoptic gospels were being written; even though no scriptural "render unto Caesar" admonition was added to the Mormon canon, the United States had made Caesar's claims so insistent that they could no longer be ignored. The millennium's beginning had been delayed and from thenceforth Latter-day Saints would, as they awaited that happy occurrence, have to make some accommodation to the world. In the absence of the apocalypse (which might be defined as the inauguration of permanent sacred time) the Saints would have to learn to live apocalyptically.[41] The work of Wayne Meeks, John Gager, and others makes it clear that the Christian community's negotiation of the passage out of sacred time that came at the end of the apostolic era could well have been the point at which Christianity as a religious tradition was most vulnerable.[42] Certainly it is possible to use this parallel to suggest that in Mormonism the passage from the pioneer era to the modern age was likewise a time of enormous vulnerability: some of the Saints wanted to turn backward, seeking to recapture the exhilarating experience of living in illo tempore by trying to continue to use the patriarchal order of marriage as a boundary separating the Saints from the world; while others, already impatient to get on with the business of living in the world, were ready to accommodate to the larger American pattern in religion at the expense of fundamental elements in Mormonism.

The generality of Latter-day Saints today would give God the credit for seeing the Church through this time of crisis. Two specific instances of continuing revelation can be cited to support this interpretation: the suspension of the adoption ordinance and President Joseph F. Smith's vision of the redemption of the dead. The ordinance of baptism for the dead was introduced into Mormonism in the Nauvoo period, but during the trek and the pioneer period—as the Saints waited for the advent of the millennium in which God would take the world forward (or backward) to its paradisiacal state—even the possibility of carrying the ordinances of the gospel to the dead in wholesale fashion would have, to say the least, seemed remote. Moreover, until President Smith described the process he had seen in a vision by which the dead are redeemed, the compelling necessity for so doing had not been made absolutely clear to the Saints. Comprehension of this need can be connected to the expansion of the genealogy program since the turn of the century which establishes an LDS line backward in time. The business of the trek and the pioneer period was the forging of an ethnic identity as a literal New Israel; in addition to patriarchal blessing designations of lineage, the development of close intra-Mormon kinship ties was facilitated during that time both by plural marriage and by the ordinance of adoption. But with those ties formed, the restoration of the ten tribes called for the performance of the symbolic ordinances for the dead that would tie modern families to their Hebraic ancestors. The revelations suspending the adoption ordinances and providing a vision of the redemption of the dead turned the attention of the Saints to responsibilities which, carried out in profane time, became occasions for returning periodically to sacred time through the medium of the ritual performance of sacred ordinances.[43]

The preservation of a Mormonism changed but continuous with the LDS past is, however, most importantly made possible through means less esoteric. The transfer of boundary maintenance responsibility to individuals, especially through close adherence to the Word of Wisdom and careful compliance with a clearly articulated behavioral code, has long been effected so that Latter-day Saints are constantly reminded of their chosen status by what they eat and do not eat (as Arrington and Bitton point out, the parallel with the Jewish dietary laws is instructive) and by the ways in which they behave. Moreover, since the Saints are expected to clothe themselves with special undergarments that symbolize their covenants made during the celebration of the ordinances of the endowment in the temple, they are kept ever mindful that they are God's people by what they wear as well.

Worship activity that at times seems almost mandatory in the twentieth-century Mormon world supplements the

LDS dietary, behavior, and dress codes. Just as important, and quite possibly more important, the structured maintenance of community—through priesthood, auxiliary, and youth activities, an elaborate educational program, and an extraordinary visiting teacher program—makes Saints perpetually aware that they are members of a chosen band.

Although their everyday lives are ordinarily lived out in a profane and, in very many instances, gentile world, twentieth-century Latter-day Saints still possess the means of reentering sacred time and space. By their very nature temples are sacred space, and time spent therein has a ritual sacredness attached to it. And tabernacles and ward chapels, their multiform uses to the contrary notwithstanding, are sometimes also transformed so that entering them carries Saints away from the profane world of everyday. Sundays, particularly fast Sundays, permit the regular recovery of a certain kind of sacred time, too.

Beyond that, there is another extraordinarily important way in which today's Latter-day Saints reenter sacred space and time. Certain places and events in the everyday world trigger that reentry when the spirit is truly sensitive. The reading of the history of the pioneer period; standing in Temple Square; looking up at Eagle Gate; sitting in conference when the whole community is symbolically gathered back to the center place; participating in, or even simply watching, the pioneer parade on the Twenty-fourth of July each year: these are examples of customary situations that can take modern Saints back to the mythic time when the Mormon world was fresh and new. This does not happen all the time, nor does it happen to all the Saints. But the return to the uniquely sacred time in the Utah Mormon experience happens often enough to a large enough number of Latter-day Saints to guarantee that today's Saints live out their lives in a corporate community that still stands squarely and securely in the presence of the past.

Notes

1. Mircea Eliade, *The Sacred and the Profane: The Nature of Religion*, trans. Willard R. Trask (New York: Harcourt, Brace, 1959), introduction.

2. These movements are institutionalized as subgroups of the American Academy of Religion.

3. Lawrence Foster,*Religion and Sexuality: Three American Communal Experiments of the Nineteenth Century* (New York: Oxford University Press, 1981); Mark P. Leone, *Roots of Modern Mormonism* (Cambridge: Harvard University Press, 1979).

4. A useful recent summary of the situation that reveals the extent of outside pressure figuring in the decision to stop the practice of plural marriage is E. Leo Lyman, "The Mormon Quest for Utah Statehood" (Ph.D. diss., University of California, Riverside, 1981), chapter 5.

5. Joseph R. Gusfield, *Symbolic Crusade: Status Politics and the American Temperence Movement* (Urbana: University of Illinois Press, 1963), pp. 6-7.

6. Because it was originally issued in the form of a press release declaring that accusations charging the LDS church leaders with continuing to teach, encourage, and urge the practice of polygamy were false, the Manifesto has often been treated as Exhibit A to prove that the decision to end polygamy was simply a matter of accommodating the church to American culture. The orthodox LDS position rejects this notion out of hand, holding instead that Woodruff's action was divinely inspired.

7. A historical interpretation that might be described as the "grand conspiracy" interpretation holds that a division was made between the *church* and the *priesthood* before the Manifesto was issued. This division, so the interpretation goes, made it possible for the leaders of the Church to say in all honesty that the Church was no longer teaching the practice of polygamy nor solemnizing polygamous marriages, while the practice continued through the agency of the LDS priesthood. The fact that at least two apostles who were members of the Council of the Twelve continued to contract plural marriages is regarded as evidence of conspiracy, as is evidence that George Q. Cannon extended official approval to plural marriages solemnized in Mexico after 1890. The "grand conspiracy" idea is basic to the doctrine subscribed to by most modern Mormon polygamists who continue to practice plural marriage. A recent work in which this historical interpretation is worked out is Samuel W. Taylor, *Rocky Mountain Empire: The Latter-day Saints Today* (New York: Macmillan, 1978).

8. Reed Smoot's election to the United States Senate brought about a Senate investigation of the Mormon Church so intensive and widely publicized that a reintroduction of the practice of plural marriage would have been impossible even if that had been the intent.

9. Klaus J. Hansen, *Mormonism and the American Experience* (Chicago: University of Chicago Press, 1981).

10. Historical treatments that emphasize the wealth of the Church unduly are generally superficial and tend toward exposé. Two examples are Wallace Turner, *The Mormon Establishment* (Boston: Houghton, Mifflin, 1966), and William J. Whalen, *The Latter-day Saints in the Modern Day World* (New York: John Day Company, 1964).

11. Klaus J. Hansen, *Quest for Empire: The Political Kingdom of God and the Council of Fifty in Mormon History* (East Lansing: Michigan State University Press, 1970); Leone, *Roots of Modern Mormonism*, especially chapter 7.

12. James B. Allen and Glen M. Leonard, *The Story of the Latter-day Saints* (Salt Lake City: Deseret Book, 1976), chapter 14; Leonard J. Arrington and Davis Bitton, *The Mormon Experience: A History of the Latter-day Saints* (New York: Alfred A. Knopf, 1979), chapter 13.

13. Gordon C. Thomasson, "The Manifesto Was a Victory!" *Dialogue: A Journal of Mormon Thought* 6 (Spring

1971):37-45; Taylor, *Family Kingdom* (New York: Macmillan, 1951); idem., *Rocky Mountain Empire.*

14. Almost any standard survey of American Protestantism treats the importance of the salvation experience under the rubric of revivalism. Martin Marty's *Righteous Empire* (New York: The Dial Press, 1970) is particularly useful in describing the triumph of evangelical Protestantism. See also Bernard A. Weisberger, *They Gathered at the River: The Story of the Great Revivalists and Their Impact upon Religion in America* (Boston: Little, Brown, & Co., 1958).

15. The pattern for adoption into Israel that is directly related to the LDS usage of the term is Jacob's adoption of Manasseh and Ephraim described in Genesis 48.

16. Wayne Meeks, "Social Functions of Apocalyptic," address presented in the Religious Studies Departmental Lecture Series, Indiana University, Bloomington, Ind., 13 March 1979.

17. Brigham Young et al., *Journal of Discourses,* 26 vols. (Liverpool: Richards et al., 1854-87), 26:175.

18. The desire mankind has to live "in the beginning" is fully described, with examples drawn from many different cultures, in the second chapter of Eliade's *The Sacred and the Profane*, entitled "Sacred Time and Myths."

19. Paul D. Hanson, *The Dawn of Apocalyptic* (Philadelphia: Fortress Press, 1975).

20. Although precise comparison of emphases on Old and New Testament apocalyptic found either in evangelical Protestantism or Mormonism is exceedingly difficult, an indicator that can serve a comparative purpose is a comparison of index references to the books of Daniel and Revelation in *Quest for Empire*, Klaus J. Hansen's study of millennialism in Mormonism, and *Redeemer Nation: The Idea of America's Millennial Role* (Chicago: University of Chicago Press, 1968) by Ernest Lee Tuveson. Hansen's work has a single reference to the

Book of Revelation in the index, while the index to Tuveson's work has, in addition to two separate single-page references, "*passim*" references to sections nine and eighteen pages in length. The Hansen index has seven references to the Book of Daniel, while the Tuveson index has only two. Another indicator of the extent to which the Saints turned to the Old Testament apocalyptic rather than the new is the index of the 26 volumes of the *Journal of Discourses*, which contains transcriptions of sermons given during the pioneer period by principal LDS leaders. This index contains only one reference to the book of Revelation, but multiple references to the Book of Daniel.

21. Alma R. Blair, "Reorganized Church of Jesus Christ of Latter Day Saints: Moderate Mormonism," in F. Mark McKiernan et al., *The Restoration Movement: Essays in Mormon History* (Lawrence: Coronado Press, 1973) pp. 207-30.

22. In a highly respected but now somewhat dated sociological study of *The Mormons* (Chicago: University of Chicago Press, 1957), Thomas F. O'Dea described the Latter-day Saints as "a peculiarly American *subculture*," [italics mine] as well as "a peculiarly American religion." The interpretation being put forward in this paper goes beyond O'Dea's conclusion to suggest that the Latter-day Saints, by virtue of a common paradigmatic experience as well as isolation, have acquired an ethnic identity so distinct that it sets the Saints apart in much the same fashion that their ethnic identity sets the Jews apart.

23. Exclusive claims were made by many religious groups in nineteenth-century America, but for the most part other claims were grounded in New Testament theology, especially as articulated in the Pauline letters. While there can be no question about whether the Mormons are Christian (the LDS Articles of Faith begin "We believe in God, the Eternal Father, and in His Son, Jesus Christ," and include the statement, "We believe that the first principles and ordinances of the Gospel are: first, Faith in the Lord Jesus Christ"), their position is more closely aligned to that held by the Apostle Peter before the Jerusalem Conference.

24. Guilford Dudley III, *Religion on Trial: Mircea Eliade and His Critics* (Philadelphia: Temple University Press, 1977), p. 67.

25. Richard Rubenstein, *Power Struggle* (New York: Scribners, 1974).

26. Richard Rubenstein, *After Auschwitz: Radical Theology and Contemporary Judaism* (Indianapolis: Bobbs-Merrill, 1966), pp. 131-42. The quotation comes from page 133.

27. Rubenstein's argument about the impact of the return to Israel on Judaism is much influenced by Freudian psychology. In using his work for the purpose of drawing an analogy to assist in explicating nineteenth-century Mormon experience, I have made no effort to extend the analogy to develop the psychoanalytic dimension of theology of the Latter-day Saints.

28. Leone, *Roots of Modern Mormonism*, p. 25. Leone's summary of the situation in the second half of the nineteenth century reads: "Mormons defined, more or less on their own terms, the relationship that they would have with the rest of the world, principally the United States. These years saw Mormonism become a working society, growing to maturity through its capacity to handle a harsh environment. With a fully operating government and a dynamic economy centrally managed along socialist lines, Mormonism strove to create internal self-sufficiency, and to a remarkable degree it succeeded. These years were in many ways Mormonism's finest. The church ran itself according to its own lights and, in so doing, became the only American utopia ever to turn itself into a state."

29. In addition to Leone's work, the economic and social independence of nineteenth-century Mormonism is described in both *The Story of the Latter-day Saints* by Allen and Leonard, and *The Mormon Experience* by Arrington and Bitton.

30. Dale Morgan, "The State of Deseret," *Utah Historical Quarterly*, 8 (1940): 64-239; Hansen, *Quest for Empire*, chapter 7; D. Michael Quinn, "American Religious Diplomacy: Scholarly Neglect and Prominent Example," unpublished essay.

31. Rubenstein, *After Auschwitz*, p. 132.

32. Leonard J. Arrington, Feramorz Y. Fox, & Dean L. May, *Building the City of God: Community & Cooperation among the Mormons* (Salt Lake City: Deseret Book, 1976).

33. This is essentially the thesis of both *Building the City of God* and Arrington's *Great Basin Kingdom: An Economic History of the Latter-day Saints, 1830-1900* (Cambridge: Harvard University Press, 1958).

34. As late as 1920, sacrament meeting attendance, for example, was still at just above 15 percent, and attendance at Melchizedek Priesthood meetings was less than 20 percent. Richard O. Cowan and Wilson K. Andersen, *The Living Church: The Unfolding of the Programs and Organization of The Church of Jesus Christ during the Twentieth Century* (Provo, Utah: Brigham Young University Printing Service, 1974), pp. 185, 190.

35. Leonard J. Arrington, "Have the Saints Always Given as Much Emphasis to the Word of Wisdom as They Do Today?" *Ensign* 7 (April 1977):32-33.

36. Descriptions of the efforts made by the Mormon community to preserve the practice of polygamy are plentiful. One of the best and most complete is Gustive O. Larson's *The "Americanization" of Utah for Statehood* (San Marino, Calif.: Huntington Library, 1971).

37. This diary entry has been reprinted many times. See, for instance, Brigham H. Roberts, *A Comprehensive History of the Church of Jesus Christ of Latter-day Saints: Century I*, 6 vols. (Salt Lake City: Deseret News Press, 1930), 6:220.

38. The change in Mormonism is the basic explanation that dissident LDS groups advance to justify their existence. See Lyle O. Wright, "Origin and Development of the Church of the Firstborn of the Fulness of Times" (Master's thesis, Brigham Young University, 1963); and Russell R. Rich, *Those Who Would Be Leaders: Offshoot of Mormonism*, 2d ed. (Provo, Utah: Extension Publications, Division of Continuing Education, Brigham Young University, 1967).

39. Leon Festinger et al., *When Prophecy Fails* (Minneapolis: University of Minnesota Press, 1956), p. 28.

40. Membership statistics are available in the Church almanacs published annually by the *Deseret News*. I am grateful to Professor Ned Hill for assistance in figuring growth rates.

41. That the necessity of adjusting to a world wherein Caesar reigned was a crucial factor in causing the New Testament Saints to "reenter time" was first suggested to me by the Reverend George Davis. I have—more or less directly— adopted his words to express the idea that, instead of living in the apocalyptic kingdom, the Saints had to learn to live apocalyptically.

42. Meeks, "Social Functions of Apocalyptic"; Gager, *Kingdom and Community: The Social World of Early Christianity* (Englewood Cliffs, N.J.: Prentice-Hall, 1975).

43. James B. Allen, "Line upon Line . . ." *Ensign* 9 (July 1979):32-39.

2

A Demographic Portrait of the Mormons, 1830-1980

Dean L. May

For some time students of the Latter-day Saint experience have been forced to rely upon rather gross guesses of membership, particularly for the nineteenth century. Now, applying the techniques of modern demographic analysis, Dean L. May, Assistant Professor of History and Director of the Center for Historical Population Studies at the University of Utah, has provided rather careful estimates of Latter-day Saint population together with an analysis of the meaning of the statistics.

Some of the statistical data seem rather startling and other estimates seem to confirm what we have previously believed. If, as he indicates, approximately 60 percent of the Nauvoo population went west, then fully 40 percent remained in Nauvoo—a much larger percentage than we have formerly believed. Nearly two-fifths of those who went west were British converts. If his estimates are correct, it seems probable that a large percentage of the native American Latter-day Saints remained in the Nauvoo area instead of following Brigham Young and the Twelve to the West. In addition, his data—that the overwhelming percentage of the population of Utah communities such as those in Cache Valley consisted of immigrants and their children— confirm both this estimate and the nineteenth-century stereotype of Mormons as predominantly European immigrants. His data on the decline of the percentage of Mormons in Utah's population from 1870 through 1920 are generally known, but it bears repeating that Patrick Edward Connor's prediction proved somewhat accurate.

Demography is one of those unfortunate disciplines that has suffered the perilous fate of becoming fashionable. Everyone talks about it, every academic department feels they should have at least one, and a good many people call themselves demographers who had not heard the word five years ago. A few weeks ago I received in the mail a simple name and address form labeled "demographic information sheet."

In fact, demography is a highly technical and specialized discipline. The more general concerns of the field are comprehended in the so-called "balancing equation" of demography

$$P_t - P_o = B - D + I - O$$

where P_t is the population at the end of a stated period, P_o at the beginning, B is for births, D is for deaths, I is for in-migration, and O is for out-migration. In the simplest terms, the demographer is trying to understand the dynamics of change in human populations. If he knows the number of births, deaths, in-migrants, and out-migrants for a given area and a given period of time, and the population at the beginning of the period, he can readily compute the population at the end of the period.

It sounds simple—in fact, tediously obvious. But doing it is a different matter. Take the Mormon situation, for example. By the terms of the equation we could substitute some 5 million for P_t, the number 6 for P_o, and then, in order to understand how the Mormons have grown over the last 150 years, we need only add up total births, subtract deaths, then add the difference between in-migration and out-migration. Unfortunately, there is no reliable way to measure how many births or deaths took place among the Mormons in the intervening years since 1830. Conversion presents problems as well, for with Mormons it would have to be seen as a special form of in-migration, and excommunication a special form of out-migration; and then how do we deal with those who aren't excommunicated but just drop out? The whole situation becomes very sticky at the outset, certainly not amenable to any quick or easy solution.

Having said all this, I will digress somewhat from this bare-bones statement of the demographer's concerns to ask and explore questions about the relationship of what little we know about Mormon demography to what we may or may not know about the social and cultural life of the Mormons. The balancing equation might help provide an outline for our explorations, however, for in all its terms—of birth, death, in-migration, and out-migration— the Mormons contrast rather sharply with the general population. Mormons are more fertile than most people around them; Mormons have a lower death rate than other Americans. Mormon migration—whether we consider it in the traditional sense of spatial migration or as religious migration in and out of identification with a particular group—has been shaped by idiosyncratic factors that make it unusual if not unique. My aim is obviously not to discuss all we know of each of these topics, but rather to point out certain aspects of what we know as they relate to the broader question of what Mormons are.

There are few benchmarks in early Mormon history that provide a clear fix on how many Mormons there were at any given point. Indeed, the first systematic series of data on the number of Mormons worldwide dates from 1879, apparently a product of Brigham Young's reorganization of 1877. Before that time most reports on the Mormon population were sporadic or partial censuses or highly unreliable impressionistic estimates of various observers. Moreover, Mormons had a vexing habit of avoiding federal censuses—the Kirtland, Missouri, and Nauvoo migrations being neatly timed to make the federal census of little use in reconstructing the Mormon population.

There were by the end of 1830 Mormon congregations in New York and Ohio numbering perhaps two- to five-hundred souls. Joseph Smith reported 70 in New York,[1] and

Parley P. Pratt reported baptizing 127 in Kirtland on his way west in 1830. This number, Pratt wrote, "soon increased to one thousand."[2] Marvin S. Hill, C. Keith Rooker, and Larry T. Wimmer have estimated the overall Kirtland population between 1830 and 1840 from the number of personal property owners taxed each year. They show the population growing rapidly from just over 1,000 in 1830 to a peak of 2,500 in 1837, then declining sharply in 1838 and 1839 to a low of 1,704.[3] Milton V. Bachman has reworked the Kirtland data and found the Hill/Rooker/Wimmer estimates to be low by several hundred. We will look forward to his findings in his forthcoming volume of the sesquicentennial history of the Latter-day Saints. Given that there was a substantial proportion of non-Mormons in Kirtland, however, we can safely conclude that there were at the peak likely no more than 2,500 Mormons in the area, perhaps considerably fewer. The decline noted by Hill, Rooker, and Wimmer of 796 persons in 1838 and 1839 can largely be attributed to Mormons moving to Missouri, but non-Mormon towns in the area suffered noticeable declines as well, apparently in response to the economic crisis precipitated by the Panic of 1837. In any case the figure presents a near maximum for Mormons moving from Ohio to join Saints in Missouri in 1838 and 1839. Probably 500 to 1,000 persons so strongly identified themselves with the Mormons that they were led to join the main body of Mormons at the end of the 1830s.

By the spring of 1838 the Mormon population in Caldwell County, Missouri, is reported to have been about 4,900.[4] That figure is called into question, however, by the first count of Mormons, the Lesser Priesthood Enumeration, taken in Nauvoo in 1842. This census lists only 3,000 in the city and perhaps 1,000 in the environs—and this after 500 to 1,000 Saints from Kirtland and Canada had joined the Missouri Saints, and after the first English migrations had begun.[5] My judgment would be that the

Aaronic Priesthood took the census with less than perfect efficiency. Hamlin Cannon lists 2,989 leaving Britain in 1840, 1841, and 1842, which, if they all made it to Nauvoo, would very nearly by themselves account for the whole population enumerated by the Aaronic Priesthood.[6]

Perhaps some sense can be made of the jumble if we work backwards from the 1845 census reported in the *Times and Seasons* of November 15 showing 11,057 in Nauvoo proper and "without the limits it is supposed there is a third more." Let us assume that elastic "it is supposed" is reasonably accurate, giving a total Nauvoo-area Mormon population of 14,742. I have tried to simulate the order of growth required to reach that population in six years, counting both 1840 and 1845 (the census was in November), assuming that 90 percent of the annual British migration reached Nauvoo, and assuming a birth rate of 50 per thousand and a high death rate of 20 per thousand. If the base population of 1840 had been 4,000 and there were a non-British in-migration of 600 each year, the population would have been 14,677, or very close to that estimated in the census by the end of 1845. This only shows that an estimated 4,000 Saints leaving Missouri and 3,600 entering from the states added to an estimated 4,216 arriving in Nauvoo from England could have produced the census population of 14,742 by 1845 in the time shown with an average birthrate and a fairly high death rate.

One could adjust any of these estimations (base population, non-British in-migration, or crude rate of natural increase) upward or downward somewhat, but not greatly without straining our credulity. If the 1842 Aaronic Priesthood census were accurate it would have taken an average non-British in-migration of 1,500 persons each year from 1842 to 1845 to approximate the 1845 census figures. I thus am inclined to consider the 1842 census incomplete and to have some confidence in an initial population of 4,000 Mormons gathered to Nauvoo from Missouri and Ohio, providing the base upon which the

Mormon population grew by the end of 1845 to be approximately 14,000 or 15,000. Nauvoo experts James L. Kimball and Rowena Miller will no doubt refine and correct these estimates as their work progresses.

Estimating the number of Mormons elsewhere presents equally difficult problems. Wilford Woodruff recorded that in April 1841 there were 5,814 Saints in England.[7] The precision of the figure possibly makes it an actual count of the members. Using the same crude rate of natural increase, adding Hamlin Cannon's data on conversions and deducting his recorded out-migration figures and 10 percent for apostasy, the British membership would have grown to 9,882 by the end of 1846. If we were to allow another 1,000 for Saints elsewhere in Europe and 5,000 for Saints elsewhere in North America, the total Church membership would have been 30,882. I would be comfortable with a working estimate of 30,000 for the whole Church population at the time the wagons began to pull out into the mire of the Iowa countryside in 1846, half of them resident in the Nauvoo area.

The next estimates based on actual counts are from the 1850 censuses for Pottawattamie County, Iowa, and Utah. They list 7,828 for Pottawattamie County and 11,380 for Utah.[8] Lowell C. Bennion and Marilyn Wagner in separate studies have found evidence of redundancy in the 1850 Utah census, with some persons being counted twice—as residents of settled areas and of new colonies. Moreover, it is impossible to know precisely how many gentiles were in Utah and Pottawattamie County at the time. The best method I have devised for making some sense of the early Utah population begins with the annual immigrant company reports and takes them to a bishops' census reported in April 1853, representing the population of the territory after the great 1852 migration had reached Utah. Table I shows the various possibilities I have computed with the numbers recorded in the 1850 federal census and the 1853 bishops' census. The table indicates which population levels were feasible, working from known data and several reasonable options for unknown data. For example, the reader may see the 10,092 estimate as closest to the 1850 federal census report, but in accepting it he must accept a 15 percent rate of under-reporting of in-migration and a 0 percent rate of out-migration.

I have used 3.5 percent per year crude rate of natural increase for these calculations, somewhat higher than Wayne Wahlquist has used, but representing more accurately, I believe, the population of Utah at the time.[9] Clearly, as column B shows, the in-migration is under-reported, for had it not been, the population at the end of 1852 with no out-migration would have been nearly 2,000 short of the bishops' report, which is most likely to err in underreporting rather than overreporting the Latter-day Saint population of the territory. A 10 percent estimate of underreporting of in-migration is likewise unlikely as it gives us 251 persons less at the end of the period than the bishops' count—even if there had been no out-migration. The estimate in cell 32D, representing a 15 percent underreporting of in-migration and 1 percent out-migration, is exactly the same as the bishops' count—rather too close, I would judge, to allow for some under-reporting by the bishops. Moreover, our winning number must have a reasonable correspondence with the 1850 census. The 1850 estimate with the same assumptions, cell 20D, is 1,532 short of the federal census, a large but perhaps not impossible error in overreporting the 1850 population. For these estimates to be acceptable, however, we must assume a 1 percent or smaller rate of out-migration, which is to say in a population of 10,000 no more than 100 per year could have left Utah for California or to return to the states. There were no records kept of out-migration, though we know from many sources that a fair amount of such migration did take place. I ultimately find the 1 percent or fewer out-migration unsatisfying and

TABLE I

Estimate of Mormon
Population in Utah at 3.5%
Crude Rate of Natural Increase*

Census Reports	Year	Rate Out-migr.	A Recorded Migration	B Pop. Est. With 3.5% Inc. Only	C If Inmigr. 10% Under-registered	D If Inmigr. 15% Under-registered	E If Inmigr. 20% Under-registered	F If Inmigr. 25% Under-registered
1847	1	0%	1,637	1,694	1,864	1,948	2,033	2,118
	2	1%			1,845	1,929	2,013	2,097
	3	2%			1,826	1,909	1,992	2,076
	4	3%			1,808	1,890	1,972	2,054
	5	5%			1,771	1,851	1,931	2,012
	6	10%			1,677	1,754	1,830	1,906
1848	7	0%	2,408	4,246	4,671	4,882	5,095	5,307
	8	1%			4,605	4,814	5,023	5,233
	9	2%			4,539	4,745	4,951	5,159
	10	3%			4,474	4,678	4,881	5,084
	11	5%			4,346	4,543	4,740	4,938
	12	10%			4,029	4,213	4,396	4,579
1849	13	0%	1,574	6,024	6,626	6,926	7,228	7,529
	14	1%			6,493	6,787	7,082	7,378
	15	2%			6,360	6,649	6,938	7,228

Year	Total	In‑mig.	No.	%	(a)	(b)	(c)	(d)	(e)
			16	3%		6,230	6,514	6,797	7,079
			17	5%		5,976	6,247	6,518	6,790
			18	10%	8,776	5,366	5,611	5,854	6,098
1850	11,380	2,456							
			19	0%		9,654	10,092	10,531	10,970
			20	1%		9,421	9,848	10,276	10,706
			21	2%		9,191	9,609	10,027	10,445
			22	3%		8,967	9,375	9,783	10,189
			23	5%		8,532	8,919	9,307	9,695
			24	10%	10,446	7,515	7,858	8,198	8,540
1851		1,316							
			25	0%		11,490	12,012	12,534	13,057
			26	1%		11,137	11,641	12,147	12,655
			27	2%		10,791	11,281	11,772	12,263
			28	3%		10,456	10,931	11,407	11,881
			29	5%		9,812	10,258	10,704	10,563
			30	10%	16,414	8,349	8,729	9,107	9,487
1852	18,306	5,413							
			31	0%		18,055	18,875	19,696	20,517
			32	1%		17,513	18,306	19,102	19,900
			33	2%		16,985	17,756	**18,529**	19,301
			34	3%		16,475	17,224	17,973	18,721
			35	5%		15,502	16,207	16,912	17,039
			36	10%		13,324	13,930	14,534	15,140

*Sources: U.S. Census returns for 1850 and "Reports of Bishops in Utah Territory," LDS Historical Department. The author was directed to the latter reports by William G. Hartley of the Joseph Fielding Smith Historical Institute, Lowell C. Bennion of Humboldt State University, California and Ronald G. Watt of the LDS Church Historical Department and gratefully acknowledges their assistance in this project. The recorded in‑migration is from data compiled by Gladys Noyce and other members of the LDS Church Historical Department and published in the *Deseret News 1977 Church Almanac* (Salt Lake City: Deseret News, 1977): pp. 278‑292.

am forced into column E for a more reasonable choice. It seems most likely that in-migration was on the average underreported by 20 percent and that out-migration was about 2 percent. Such a conclusion would lead us to cell 33E for an estimate of 18,529 in 1852—close enough in my judgment to the bishops' count to be reasonable, and 10,027 for 1850—about 1,353 short of the federal census figure. The table makes it clear that out-migration could not have been greater than 3 percent without accepting a higher than 20 percent rate of underreporting of in-migration, which would seem most unlikely.

My choice of the estimates, then, is in the next table. It shows the 1850 census overreporting the Mormon population by 1,353, allowing considerable but reasonable margin for redundancy and gentile presence in the territory. It shows an early 1853 population of 18,529, including the great migration of 1852. If this estimate is close to the actual and we reckon the 7,828 Pottawattamie County

TABLE II
Estimated Utah Population
at 3.5% crude rate of Natural Increase
20% Underregistration of in-migration
2% out-migration

Year	Population	Census	
1847	1,992		
1848	4,951		
1849	6,983		
1850	10,027	11,380	U.S. Census 1,353 Overreported
1851	11,772		
1852	18,529	18,306	Bishop Census 223 Underreported

Source: Computations from Table I and U.S. printed census returns.

population of 1850 as a minimal 90 percent Latter-day Saint, then we can look back on Nauvoo and produce a reasonable estimate of how many Saints from Nauvoo came west by 1853. My figures suggest a total western U.S. population of Mormons in 1850 of 17,072, with 41 percent, nearly half, still living in western Iowa.

How many of that 17,000 were recent arrivals from England? We have already accounted for the English migration up to 1846. From 1846 to 1852, 6,597 Mormons boarded emigrant ships in England. [10] If we assume that about 10 percent stopped along the way in New Orleans, St. Louis, or other river towns, and allow a low 3 percent rate of natural increase, we can account for 6,519 persons through English in-migration or 38 percent of the whole Mormon western population. This leaves about 10,553 who could have come west from Nauvoo, but of course a good share of them were born between 1846 and 1850.

TABLE III
English Emigration 1846-1852

Year	Departed	Less 10% Attrition	Est. Population including 3% Natural Increase
1846	50	45	46
1847	0	0	46
1848	755	680	748
1849	2078	1870	2697
1850	1612	1451	4272
1851	1370	1233	5670
1852	732	659	6519
	6597	5938	

Source: Hamlin Cannon, "Migration of English Mormons to American," *American Historical Review* 57 (April, 1947): 441.

A base population of 9,190 leaving Nauvoo could have grown to 10,550, just three under our calculated figure, by the end of 1850, even if we cut the rate of natural increase to 2 percent for the year 1846 to allow for high mortality in that year. Given that there were migrations from elsewhere in the United States to join the Mormons at Pottawattamie and the Great Salt Lake, it is not likely that more than 8,800 or from 59 to 63 percent of Nauvoo's 14 or 15 thousand followed Brigham Young west by 1850. All the American Saints coming west together with the British Saints who left England between 1846 and 1850 total about 15,397 souls, or just over half the worldwide Church membership at the time the flight from Nauvoo began. These calculations suggest that the proportions of Mormons migrating west from Nauvoo between 1846 and 1850 may have been substantially less than has been thought and that a very high proportion (38 percent) of the western U.S. Mormons were British born—persons converted under the ministry of the apostles and perhaps feeling a special loyalty to that body.

After the 1850s we have no clear readings on the population of the Mormons until 1870, when the first reasonably complete series of annual statistical reports appears.[11] Even then the data are very difficult to use and compare with other sources, as they report all Church membership only in 1880, and thereafter do not include mission reports, at least in the same listing. I have calculated the Utah Church population to 1860, using migration data as 20 percent underregistered, a 3.5 percent rate of natural increase, and a 2 percent out-migration rate, and find the estimated population, including the 1860 in-migrants, to be 41,303. Given the general underregistration of federal censuses after 1850 I find the estimate not unlikely. It is 5,743 short of Wahlquist's 47,046 estimate of total Utah population for the same year, and some 1,030 greater than the 40,273 federal census count. If Walquist's territorial estimate is correct, Mormons accounted for 88 percent of the territorial population.

These data give us some insight into another interesting question concerning the Mormon population—or at least the Utah Mormon population—that of how prophetic Colonel Patrick Connor was in suggesting that an influx of gentiles would attend the opening of the precious metal mining industry sufficient to diminish if not overcome Mormon control of the territory. Comparing Church membership data for Utah with the federal census, we find that eighteen years after Fort Douglas was established and eleven years after the railroad made large-scale mining feasible the Mormons had dropped from our 1860 estimate of 88 percent of the population to 79 percent. This figure declined sharply to 66 percent in 1890.[12] Mormons accounted for 67 percent in 1900, 61 percent in 1910, and reached their low point at 55 percent in 1920. Thereafter the proportion of Mormons rose steadily a few points a year, reaching a twentieth-century high of 71.5 in 1970, according to data compiled independently by Joseph L. Lyon and Lowell C. Bennion. Connor's hope, I would judge, was realized, though more slowly and not to the degree he had planned. And finally it was the mining of industrial metals (such as lead and copper) and of coal that brought the Mormons to near-minority status in 1920, not the precious metal industry. The 1970 data show a total of 1,059,273 in Utah, with 757,036 or 71.5 percent Mormons. County percentages range from 21.9 percent Mormon in Grand County to 93.5 percent in Wayne County. Apparently the LDS records used in this computation do not exaggerate the proportion of Mormons, as random polls that ask for religious preference consistently find 75 to 78 percent of adults in Utah reporting their religious preference as LDS. Since Mormons have almost twice the birthrate of non-Mormons in Utah, this figure is quite remarkable.[13]

How, then, can we summarize this bare profile of Mormon growth over the last 150 years? If my estimation procedures are close, the numbers are considerably less than is often thought, at least for the Nauvoo and early Utah period. The 4,000 leaving Missouri to settle Nauvoo is not far from contemporary estimates. The peak population of 14,000 to 15,000 for Nauvoo is also close to what has been thought, but the estimation of 8,800 leaving Nauvoo to go west is lower than many have assumed. The 30,000 worldwide population in 1846 is substantially less than contemporary *New York Sun* accounts (in *Times and Seasons* 6:1052), which suggest 57,000 to 200,000. It is clear that the 1850 population was over-enumerated in the federal census. I am surprised at the small out-migration to California and elsewhere permitted by my estimates. I quite frankly began these exercises expecting to find the territory a wide-open sieve on the California side, an expectation that clearly was not realized. Finally, I am impressed with how large a component the English and their children were of the whole western Church population by 1850—apparently already making up nearly 40 percent of the Church membership.

Now let me proceed to point out one or two important aspects of the components of Mormon growth over the last 150 years. Of all distinctive aspects of Mormon demography, high fertility has been most often noticed and commented upon. This much is known of Mormon fertility. Mormons had fertility rates approaching natural fertility until the 1870s, when evidence of fertility control becomes evident in the data. Since that time Mormon fertility has tended to follow national trends, though at a higher level. The influence of peer groups, which probably brought fertility decline in the 1870s, is evident today as Mormons living among non-Mormon populations have higher fertility than their non-Mormon neighbors, though less fertility than Mormons living in predominantly LDS areas.[14] Mormon fertility remains high—indeed it increased during the late 1970s and the Mormon crude birth rate is now twice the national average.

Graph I

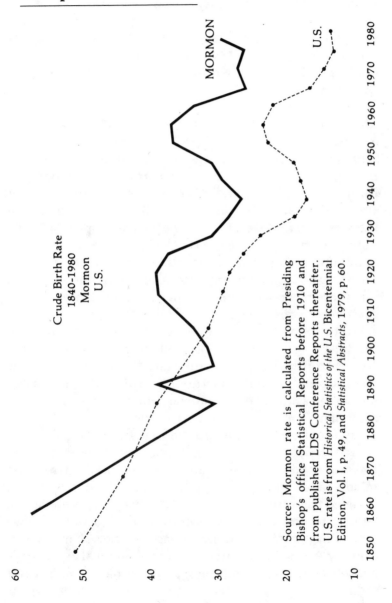

Crude Birth Rate
1840-1980
Mormon
U.S.

Source: Mormon rate is calculated from Presiding Bishop's office Statistical Reports before 1910 and from published LDS Conference Reports thereafter. U.S. rate is from *Historical Statistics of the U.S. Bicentennial Edition*, Vol. I, p. 49, and *Statistical Abstracts*, 1979, p. 60.

Graph I indicates how the Mormon crude birthrate has changed over the last 150 years. Before 1895 we are estimating annual birthrates from semiannual reports, a risky business since fertility is seasonal, or at least was in the nineteenth century. After 1895 the reports are somewhat better, though I am led to wonder if the lower fertility in the 1880s, 1890s, and 1910s is not a statistical artifact. After 1910 we see a clear parallel between Mormon and national birthrates, though there are never fewer than six points separating the two. In 1977 the Mormon crude birthrate was reported as 30.7 compared to a national rate of 15.4.[15] It is interesting that this maintenance of higher birthrates has continued in spite of increasing affluence and educational status among the Mormon people generally. While the fertility of other traditionally high fertility groups has dropped as socioeconomic status rises, that of the Mormons persists.

The interesting question is: Why does Mormon fertility maintain itself at such high levels? Numerous studies have noted high fertility among American frontier populations, but there is also a significant decline after the first generation to levels close to the national average.[16] Mormon fertility remains high, one suspects, not because of teachings against limitation, but perhaps because they were a frontier people at a time doctrines and ceremonies were strongly taught portraying parenthood as a paramount blessing of both mortal and celestial lives. One argument for this point of the view stems from the attitude of Mormons toward children. In 1960 Phillip Aries caused considerable comment by pointing out that attitudes toward children have changed dramatically from the middle ages and early modern times, when children mingled freely in adult society and were seen as miniature adults, to the nineteenth-century view of children as occupying a special position and place in society. Nineteenth-century Americans treated children somewhat as one does a darling spaniel—pampering and petting them, but not permitting them in adult society or taking them seriously as individuals until they reached an appropriate level of maturity. [17] Some have seen the Mormon fondness for children as a direct heritage of this nineteenth-century predilection, and I would submit that in part it is, but only in part.[18] Beginning with the visit of William Chandless in 1855 and continuing through *Utah Holiday* magazine in 1975, non-Mormon visitors to Deseret country have kept up a running commentary on the behavior of Mormon children which, though sometimes derogatory, presents nonetheless a common theme. [19]

These observers maintain that Mormon children are doted upon, are present and accepted in adult society, and are not taught to know their place. They are assertive, bold, even brassy, and do not respect adults. I have not researched sufficiently broadly to offer conclusions with great confidence, but I wonder if we do not see in Mormondom a strange combination of the indulgence characteristic of the nineteenth century and the acceptance of children as adults common to an earlier time. Mormon children are doted upon, but equally importantly, they are invited into adult society, as almost every non-Mormon attending Mormon church services has noted. They are accepted in adult society and recognized as individuals from an early time—given more liberties and accorded more trust than is generally the case in contemporary American society.

All of this can be tied, I suspect, both to historical experience and doctrinal roots. The Mormon doctrinal stress on the spiritual maturity and eternal importance of the individual, including the youngest of children, has helped perpetuate among them attitudes toward children that once were widespread but subsequently almost disappeared in most of nineteenth-century America. It is a persuasive argument for how important the persistence of older traditions can be when they are locked into a provincial people at a critical time. I will comment on this later, but I see in a similar manner contemporary Mormon fertility as an artifact of their having been a frontier people and then being prevented by a provincial self-consciousness from dropping frontier values and habits, especially in those areas where doctrine and belief reinforce the frontier condition.

I have deliberately avoided discussion of polygamy as it relates to fertility, but one observation might be appropriate. Those studies that see an inverse relationship between fertility per woman and polygamy, an effect noted by several researchers, tend to derive from low fertility elite segments of the population and have not considered the effect of polygamy on fertility in the aggregate.[20] That is to say that polygamy undoubtedly had the effect of taking into marriage women who would otherwise have remained infertile. My guess is that as more refined studies take these into consideration we will find that polygamy enhanced rather than depressed aggregate fertility.

Another common observation on Mormon fertility is the suggestion that the absence of husbands on missions lowered fertility. Obviously, in those individual instances it did, but since the 1840s the proportion of Mormon men on missions has never reached even half of 1 percent of the whole Church membership. Thus the percentage of Mormon men on missions was seldom enough to be of great statistical significance.[21]

One other point pertaining to the components of Mormon growth is deserving of mention. From the Church's inception until about 1880, the major portion of new members each year apparently came from convert baptisms. The only nineteenth-century listing that I can find of child baptisms and convert baptisms churchwide was for 1880. It indicates that 3,042 children and 3,606 adults were baptized during the year, the great portion of adult converts (2,286) coming from Europe.[22] It would seem likely that the Church in the 1880s was about to enter an era of some eighty years when the bulk of its growth would be internal, pulling itself up by the bootstrap of a numerous Mormon progeny. When such data appeared again in 1925 the ratio of child baptisms to convert baptisms had changed significantly—from roughly equal to more than double (225 to 100). The same ratio persisted into 1930 but then dropped sharply in 1935 (189 to 100). During the war the ratio leapt dramatically (325 to 100), obviously because of curtailment of European mission activity. Except for the war years, the trend until 1955 was toward a balance between the two. Converts began to outnumber child baptisms at some point between 1955 and 1960. From that time on the ratios drop consistently to a low of 41.4 to 100 in 1979—that is, 41 child baptisms for every 100 convert baptisms, reversing the 1925 ratio.[23] Mormon fertility remains high but can no longer compete with missionary zeal in its share of overall Church growth. And it remains high in part because Church attitudes and historical circumstances have mutually reinforced positive attitudes toward children and childbearing. This accent on the positive seems to work—at least among the Mormons.

Mormon death rates are as notable for being low as Mormon birthrates are for being high. It is unfortunate that we have no series of data with which to test the oft-stated hypothesis that Mormon mortality was low in crossing the plains compared with that of other overland migrants. No doubt Milton V. Backman and James L. Kimball are developing death data from their work on Kirtland and Nauvoo. The first death statistics I have been able to find come from a Church census of 1852, though the federal census for 1850 listed a notoriously high death rate of 21 per thousand for Utah territory in that year, a statistic Mormon critics fairly leapt upon and which was corrected in the 1860 census, either by better health or by sharper statisticians.

I have used Church data, problematic though they may be, and find them to run in a consistent and plausible

Graph II

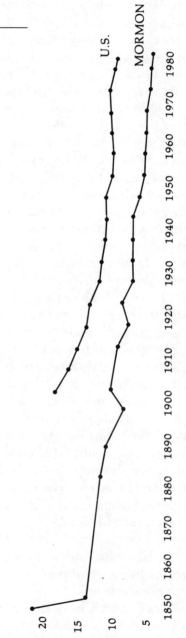

Crude Death Rates
1850-1977
Mormons
U.S.

Sources: Presiding Bishop's Office statistical reports before 1910. Thereafter, LDS General Conference Reports. Historical Statistics of the United States, Bicentennial Edition, p. 59; Statistical Abstracts after 1970.

series after the box end on the left that marks the 1850 census. It is difficult to explain why the Mormon death rate is lower in the nineteenth century than the national average, except to observe that Utah's urban centers did not have the high concentrations of populations found elsewhere in the United States that served to reduce the national average.[24] Nineteenth-century Mormons were not noted for their careful observance of the Word of Wisdom. Such observance is apparantly the main reason for the present low death rates among their descendants. Joseph L. Lyon and others have studied this phenomenon carefully, and I wish here only to make allusion to their report in the Autumn 1979 *Dialogue*. This report, showing incidence of cancer, carefully standardized for age and other factors, among LDS and non-LDS persons in Utah, indicates that in most types of cancer, including those of sites that should not be affected by tobacco or alcohol, Mormons have a substantially lower incidence than non-Mormons living in Utah.[25] These and other data on Mormon health add up to an expectation of life at birth for Mormon men five years longer than for non-Mormon men and three years longer for Mormon women than for non-Mormon women. These studies do not, however, consider the likely positive effects of Mormon health practices on pregnancy, childbirth, and birth defects.

I have already noted the high proportion of English Saints in the Mormon Church by 1850. I would like to draw upon work done by Charles M. Hatch pertaining to Cache Valley in the nineteenth century to make a point about the cultural importance of the high proportion of foreign-born in Utah. A common charge of nineteenth-century anti-Mormons was that the Saints harbored, in a day of general xenophobia, a high proportion of foreign-born who, in coming to Utah from their native lands, had never been exposed to American values and thus were susceptible to the less individualistic Mormon culture. In fact, however, in 1860 the Cache Valley population was about two-thirds American born. In 1870 62 percent were American born, just under two-thirds, and about the same proportion prevailed in 1880. So why all the fuss? The data indicate a fairly consistent pattern of large American-born majorities who presumably set the social, religious, and cultural tone of Cache Valley towns in the nineteenth century. A closer look, however, reveals a far more complicated picture. Population pyramids are commonly used to graph the structure of a population, revealing nuances the aggregate figures often conceal. A high birthrate or high crime rate, for example, may be a product of how young or old the population as a whole is, rather than of the social habits peculiar to the group. Population pyramids give us a clear and immediate picture of age structure. The pyramids for Cache County in 1860, 1870, and 1880, for example, show the broad base characteristic of high fertility populations, a sizable group of young and early middle-aged adults and a sharp pinching in the 40 and older categories, revealing this to be generally a young people, as was common in American frontier areas.

We have modified the population pyramid, however, to show, in the shaded inside area, the age structure of the foreign-born population. There are few children in the shaded areas because, of course, most of the children, except for those of very recent immigrants, were born in America. The shaded pyramid reveals clearly that the foreign-born population was concentrated in the older age categories; that from 20 upwards the proportion of foreign born exceeds that of the U. S. born substantially. This phenomenon, clearly evident in 1860, is if anything more pronounced in the 1870 population and persists strongly in 1880. Thus, if a time machine would permit us to look in on a Wellsville or Hyrum street anytime between 1860 and 1880, almost every adult we would greet would be foreign-born, either British or Scandinavian.

Where, then, would be the two-thirds American majority suggested by the aggregate data? They are

Graph III

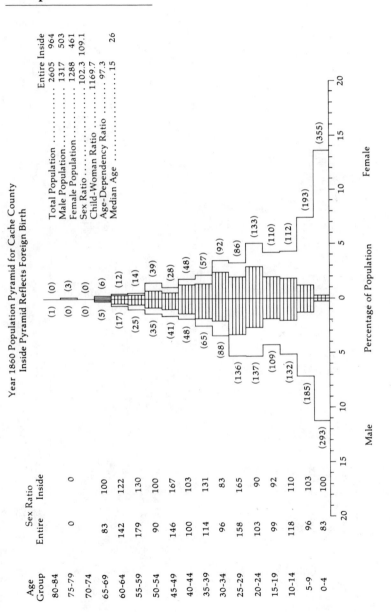

Year 1860 Population Pyramid for Cache County
Inside Pyramid Reflects Foreign Birth

	Entire	Inside
Total Population	2605	964
Male Population	1317	503
Female Population	1288	461
Sex Ratio	102.3	109.1
Child-Woman Ratio	1169.7	
Age-Dependency Ratio	97.3	
Median Age	15	26

Age Group	Sex Ratio Entire	Inside
80-84	0	0
75-79		
70-74		
65-69	83	100
60-64	142	122
55-59	179	130
50-54	90	100
45-49	146	167
40-44	100	103
35-39	114	131
30-34	96	83
25-29	158	165
20-24	103	90
15-19	99	92
10-14	118	110
5-9	96	103
0-4	83	100

Graph IV

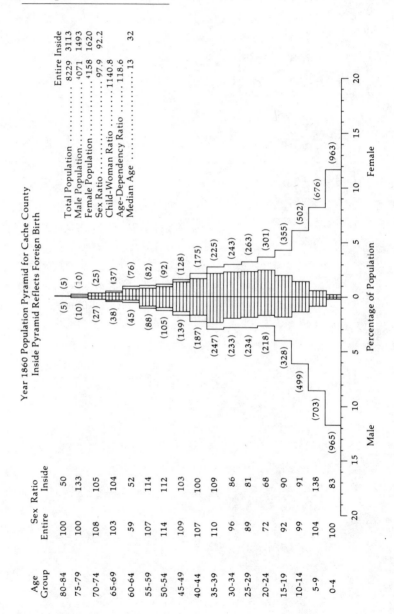

Year 1860 Population Pyramid for Cache County
Inside Pyramid Reflects Foreign Birth

	Entire	Inside
Total Population	8229	3113
Male Population	4071	1493
Female Population	4158	1620
Sex Ratio	97.9	92.2
Child-Woman Ratio	1140.8	
Age-Dependency Ratio	118.6	
Median Age	13	32

Age Group	Sex Ratio Entire	Inside
80-84	100	50
75-79	100	133
70-74	108	105
65-69	103	104
60-64	59	52
55-59	107	114
50-54	114	112
45-49	109	103
40-44	107	100
35-39	110	109
30-34	96	86
25-29	89	81
20-24	72	68
15-19	92	90
10-14	99	91
5-9	104	138
0-4	100	83

Graph V

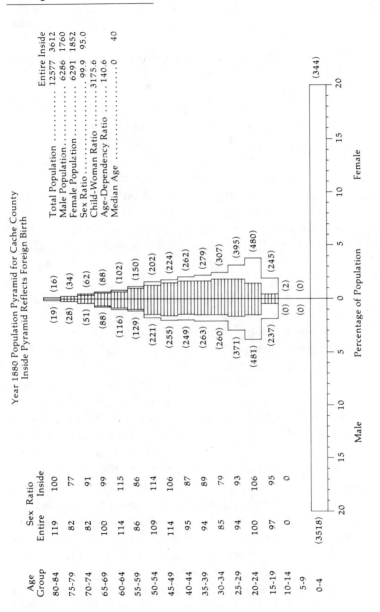

Year 1880 Population Pyramid for Cache County
Inside Pyramid Reflects Foreign Birth

	Entire	Inside
Total Population	12577	3612
Male Population............	6286	1760
Female Population..........	6291	1852
Sex Ratio	99.9	95.0
Child-Woman Ratio	3175.6	
Age-Dependency Ratio	140.6	
Median Age	0	40

Age Group	Sex Ratio				
	Entire	Inside			
80-84	119	100	(19)	(16)	
75-79	82	77	(28)	(34)	
70-74	82	91	(51)	(62)	
65-69	100	99	(88)	(88)	
60-64	114	115	(116)	(102)	
55-59	86	86	(129)	(150)	
50-54	109	114	(221)	(202)	
45-49	114	106	(255)	(224)	
40-44	95	87	(249)	(262)	
35-39	94	89	(263)	(279)	
30-34	85	79	(260)	(307)	
25-29	94	93	(371)	(395)	
20-24	100	106	(481)	(480)	
15-19	97	95	(237)	(245)	
10-14	0	0	(0)	(2)	
5-9	0	0	(0)	(0)	
0-4	(3518)			(344)	

Percentage of Population

Male   Female

virtually all children under the age of fifteen. As the population grows older the unshaded line representing American born becomes a thin veneer, the great bulk of the population being recent European immigrants to the Mormon Zion.[26]

At first glance one might conclude from this that the tone of society in Utah (as many nativist critics of Utah in the late nineteenth century suggested) *was* set by foreigners—persons alien to American traditions. Undoubtedly, the contributions of the European population to the cultural heritage of Cache Valley have been greater than is often supposed. But nonetheless, most immigrants came to Zion with a heart prepared—eager to abandon Babylon and to learn from those having priesthood authority and status within the Mormon kingdom. Social, cultural, and religious norms were set by this American elite—those who taught the Mormon gospel in Europe, arranged the voyage to America, directed the overland journey, and welcomed the incoming Saints.

If life in nineteenth-century Mormon towns seemed un-American to visitors from the East, the fault (if fault it was) lay with the old Mormons and not the new. They were the most influential shapers of Utah society. This observation may perhaps make a point worth noting for Mormons in the late twentieth century. The changes brought about by conversion and full participation in Mormon faith are profound. Moreover, in the past the old Mormons, if you will, have at times been a minority in the Church, yet their value system has for the most part been successfully imparted to those who enter the faith. Growth brings its challenges, but one suspects the Deseret Mormon is not likely in the near future to become extinct. Deseret Mormons still command a numerical majority in the Church, as Lowell C. Bennion and Dean Louder have noted, but more importantly, they dominate culturally.[27]

I remember as an experiment asking the teenage daughter of an English regional representative to name the presidents of the Latter-day Saint Church. She did so without hesitation right back to Joseph Smith. I then asked her to name the monarchs of Britain going back as far as possible. She could not get beyond Elizabeth II. The incident argues for the great power of Mormonism to "traditionalize" (to use Brigham Young's term) the convert population into identification with the Saints even above national loyalties and to adopt values and points of view taught by significant others sent out from Church head-quarters—whether missionaries, mission presidents, or General Authorities.

All of this becomes very interesting when we note that perhaps some of the cultural traits of the Deseret Mormons are in fact as much heirlooms of the nineteenth-century historical experience as of Church doctrine and principle. Perry Miller, who thought much about the nature of provincial societies and their relationship to the parent society, offered a profound insight in his *The New England Mind from Colony to Province.* "Recurrently the mind of America falls into isolation: axioms brought to this country—Puritanism, the social contract, Romanticism—and here successfully tried out, have, by the time the American experiment is completed, ceased to be meaning-ful in Europe; America is repeatedly left, so to speak, with an institution on its hands."[28]

A similiar dynamic was in operation, as Mormons were buffeted through the nineteenth century: axioms of many kinds, such as attitudes—say, toward children, or toward government influence in local affairs—found fertile root among the Mormons and then were left upon their hands as institutions, institutions that now go out of Deseret to all parts of the world as part and parcel of what it means to become a Mormon. I do not presume to say whether this is good or bad. But my observations clearly indicate that the historical experience of the Mormons has helped greatly to shape Mormon society into what it is today, including fertility, mortality, and migration patterns, and that attitudes formed in the past are now being imparted to hundreds of thousands of converts from all parts of the world by messengers sent out from the heartland of Mormonism. The cultural effects of this process in the twentieth, as in the nineteenth century, are powerful and enduring upon those of all cultures who embrace Mormonism and persist in its way.

Notes

1. Joseph Smith, *History of the Church of Jesus Christ of Latter-day Saints: Period 1*, ed. B. H. Roberts, 2nd ed., 6 vols. (Salt Lake City: Deseret Book Co., 1946-50) 1:133.

2. Parley P. Pratt, *The Autobiography of Parley P. Pratt*, ed. Parley P. Pratt, Jr., 6th ed. (Salt Lake City: Deseret Book Co., 1964), p. 48.

3. Marvin S. Hill, C. Keith Rooker, and Larry T. Wimmer, "The Kirtland Economy Revisited: A Market Critique of Sectarian Economics," *Brigham Young University Studies* 17 (Summer 1977):389-482; esp. pp. 408, 410.

4. Quoted from the *History of Caldwell County* (St. Louis: National Historical Co., 1896), p. 118, in B. H. Roberts, *A Comprehensive History of the Church of Jesus Christ of Latter-day Saints*, 6 vols. (Salt Lake City: Deseret News Press, 1930) 1:425.

5. Information from the Lesser Priesthood Enumeration supplied to the author by James L. Kimball, LDS Church Historical Department, Salt Lake City, Utah.

6. M. Hamlin Cannon, "Migration of English Mormons to America," *American Historical Review* 57 (April 1947):436-55.

7. Roberts, *Comprehensive History*, 2:85.

8. U. S. manuscript census 1850 returns for Pottawattamie County, Iowa, and for the Territory of Utah.

9. See Wayne A. Wahlquist, "Population Growth in the Mormon Core Area: 1847-70," in Richard H. Jackson, ed., *The Mormon Role in the Settlement of the West*, Charles Redd Monographs in Western History, no. 9 (Provo, Utah: Brigham Young University Press, 1978): 107-33.

10. Cannon, "Migration of English Mormons," p. 441.

11. Presiding Bishop's Office Statistical Reports for the years indicated in the text, LDS Church Archives, Salt Lake City, Utah.

12. The Utah Mormon population figure is from the Presiding Bishop's Office Reports cited above; the territorial population is from the published U. S. census reports. These figures are:

Year	Territorial Population	Mormon Population	% Mormon
1880	143,963	113,828	79
1890	210,779	138,059	65
1900	276,749	186,341	67
1910	373,351	226,355	61

13. The 1920 and subsequent estimates are from unpublished calculations done independently by Joseph L. Lyon and Lowell C. Bennion using Church population records and federal census returns. The telephone polls were conducted by University of Utah scholars in a random survey for medical research.

14. See M. Skolnick et al., "Mormon Demographic History: Nuptiality and Fertility of Once-Married Couples," *Population Studies* 32 (1978):5-19; Donald W. Hastings, Charles H. Reynolds, and Ray R. Canning, "Mormonism and Birth Planning: The Discrepancy Between Church Authorities' Teachings and Lay Attitudes," *Population Studies* 26 (1972): 19-28; Brian Pitcher, Phillip R. Kunz, and Evan T. Peterson, "Residency Differentials in Mormon Fertility," *Population Studies* 28 (1974):143-51; James E. Smith and Phillip R. Kunz,

"Polygyny and Fertility in Nineteenth-Century America,"
Population Studies 30 (1976):465-80; and Judith C. Spicer and
Susan O. Gustavus, "Mormon Fertility Through Half a
Century: Another Test of the Americanization Hypothesis,"
Social Biology 21 (1974):70-76.

15. The Mormon rate is from the Presiding Bishop's
Office Statistical Reports before 1910 and from published *LDS
General Conference Reports* thereafter (normally April
Conference). The 30.7 figure is from the April 1979 *LDS
Conference Report*. The national rates through 1970 are from
U. S., Dept. of Commerce, Bureau of the Census, *Historical
Statistics of the United States: Colonial Times to 1970*, Bicentennial
Edition, Part I (Washington, D.C.: Government Printing
Office, 1975), p. 49. Thereafter in *Statistical Abstracts*, especially
1979, p. 60.

16. Merle Curti, *The Making of an American Community: A
Case Study of Democracy in a Frontier County* (Stanford,
Calif.: Stanford University Press, 1959); John Modell, "Family
and Fertility on the Indiana Frontier 1820," *American Quarterly*
23 (1971):615-34; and Richard A. Easterlin, George Alter, and
Gretchen Condran, "Farms and Farm Families in Old and New
Areas: The Northern States in 1860," in Tamara K. Hareven
and Maris A. Vinovskis, eds., *Family and Population in Nineteenth-
Century America* (Princeton, N. J.: Princeton University Press,
1978) pp. 22-85.

17. Phillip Aries, *Centuries of Childhood: A Social History of
Family Life*, trans. Robert Boldick (New York: Vintage Books,
1962). See also Bernard Wishy, *The Child and the Republic: The
Dawn of Modern America Child Nurture* (Philadelphia: University
of Pennsylvania Press, 1968).

18. Davis Bitton is among scholars who have given special
attention to these concerns. See his "Zion's
Rowdies: Growing up on the Mormon Frontier," *Utah
Historical Quarterly* 50 (Spring 1982):182-95.

19. See, for example, William Chandless, *A Visit to Salt Lake
and . . . Mormon Settlement in Utah* (London: Smith, Elder & Co.,

1857), p. 192; Elizabeth Wood Kane, *Twelve Mormon Homes* . . . (Philadelphia, 1874), pp. 25-26, 43, 49, 58, and 77; and "Letters to the Editor," *Utah Holiday* (10 November 1975):58.

   20. Among such studies are Kimball Young, *Isn't One Wife Enough?* (New York: Henry Holt & Co., 1954); and James E. Smith and Phillip R. Kunz, "Polygyny and Fertility in Nineteenth-Century America," *Population Studies* 30 (1976):465-80.

   21. Computed from data in *Church Almanac*, (Salt Lake City: Deseret News, 1977), pp. 170-71.

   22. Presiding Bishop's Office, Statistical Reports, 1880, LDS Church Archives, Salt Lake City.

   23. *LDS General Conference Reports*, April 1925 to present.

   24. Presiding Bishop's Office, Statistical Reports, LDS Church Archives; U. S. Census Bureau, *Seventh Census of the United States, 1850* (Washington: Robert Armstron, 1853), appendix, p. xii.

   25. Joseph L. Lyon and Steven Nelson, "Mormon Health," *Dialogue* 12 (Autumn 1979):61-69.

   26. Charles M. Hatch, Dean L. May, and Fon R. Brown, "The People of Cache Valley's Jensen Farm Area in the 19th Century," (Report prepared for The Ronald V. Jensen Historical Farm and Man and His Bread Museum, Utah State University, 1979), pp. 15-21.

   27. Dean R. Louder and Lowell Bennion, "Mapping Mormons Across the Modern West," in Jackson, *The Mormon Role in the Settlement of the West*, pp. 135-67.

   28. Perry Miller, *The New England Mind: From Colony to Province* (Boston: Beacon Press, 1961), p. 119.

3

For the Strength of the Hills: Imagining Mormon Country

Edward A. Geary

Many times in the past, scholars have tried to contrast the image and the reality in the existence of a particular group of people. This has led to the writing of books with such titles as "Myth and Reality." Today we realize that such a dichotomy does not really exist since the image or myth associated with a particular lifestyle is part of its reality. Thus, it is important not only that we understand the boards and bricks of a culture but that we perceive the mythological structure that provides the glue and mortar to hold the culture together.

In the following essay, presented first as a Brigham Young University Forum address 15 July 1980, Dr. Edward A. Geary, Professor of English at Brigham Young University, examines the images of Mormon country. He argues that those who believe in reclaiming the land and making it into something they perceive as beautiful love the land as much as those who believe in a wilderness ethic. Thus, the images of mountain refuge, thrift, the garden, lombardy poplars, irrigation, and a cooperative store associated with Mormon country provide the mythic substance that distinguishes Mormon culture and provides a sense of community for the Mormon people. These images are centered in the village, which was perhaps the most typical aspect of nineteenth-century Mormon life. In fact, it really does not matter whether the village is in any objective way the most Mormon of all places. What matters is that Mormons believe it was, and thus it is our understanding their perception that is most important for understanding their culture.

As the sesquicentennial of the organization of the Church, 1980 has been a year for retrospective views. Like a good many others—especially those of my own age and older—I am a native of Mormon country, the regional culture that for about a hundred years made up virtually the whole body of the Church. Today, when the majority of Church members live outside the intermountain region, and when even within the region most people live in urban surroundings instead of the traditional farm villages, the regional period is at an end. I suppose that is one reason why I want to celebrate it. At the same time I am a bit uneasy about delivering an elegy for a vanishing way of life because Mormon country has a way of tripping up anyone who takes it too seriously. On the one hand, inhabitants of Mormon country have seen their heritage, as very important, even heroic. On the other hand, they have always known in their hearts that the reality falls short of the dream, sometimes comically or tragi-comically so.

For example, St. George, Utah's Dixie, the home town of BYU's new president Jeffrey Holland, has probably glorified its pioneers beyond any other Mormon settlement. Yet through all the Dixie lore there runs a recognition that it is really a terrible place, a mistake, a place where no person in his right mind would choose to live. From the earliest times there was a comment, first attributed to George A. Smith, for whom St. George was named, and later becoming part of the J. Golden Kimball cycle: "If I had a lot in St. George and a lot in hell, I'd sell the lot in St. George and live in hell."[1] I think of that remark whenever I see the television commercials extolling St. George as an ideal place to live. I think also of the lament of George Hicks, one of the early pioneers: "May heaven help the Dixie-ite wherever he may be!"[2]

In my home town, which was one of the last places to be settled under Brigham Young's direction, people used to say, "When Brother Brigham sent settlers into Castle Valley, the Lord called him home." Over in Sanpete Valley, where the people live on carrots (they call them Sanpete bananas), they say, "Every man ought to marry a wife from Sanpete because no matter what happens she's seen worse." Every town in Mormon country has similar deflating stories that make it difficult to sustain a mood of glorification.

Another difficulty is the scope of my topic. A complete examination of regional Mormonism is far beyond the scope of this essay, and it is beyond my competence. To do it justice I would have to be a historian, geographer, sociologist, folklorist, and more. Since I am master of none of these disciplines—though I have drawn upon them all— I would like to focus on some characteristic *images* of Mormon country, elements that have made strong impressions on the imaginations of both residents and outsiders.

There were images of Mormon country before there was a Mormon country, images generated in the short-lived settlements in Ohio, and Missouri, and Illinois, and by planned settlements that were never built, such as the City of Zion. Probably the most potent image was that of a refuge for the Saints. In 1842, Joseph Smith prophesied that the Saints would "become a mighty people in the midst of the Rocky Mountains."[3] In 1844, as the end drew near in Nauvoo, Joseph proposed sending out a party to seek a new location in the West, where, as he put it in a series of striking images, "we can build a city in a day, and have a government of our own, get up into the mountains, where the devil cannot dig us out, and live in a healthful climate, where we can live as old as we have a mind to."[4] Such statements inevitably call to mind certain Biblical images of refuge, such as the much-quoted lines in Isaiah: "And it shall come to pass in the last days, that the mountain of the Lord's house shall be established in the top of the mountains, and shall be exalted above the hills; and all nations shall flow unto it."[5]

It was with such images in mind—tempered no doubt

by harsh realities but still there—that the Saints made the trek west, and it was through those images that they viewed the land when they arrived. The view was predominantly favorable, despite the well-known remark attributed to Harriet Decker Young that she would rather travel a thousand miles farther than stop in such a barren place.[6] Probably more typical was the response of William Clayton, who thought it was "one of the most beautiful valleys and pleasant places for a home for the Saints which could be found."[7] In 1849, after barely two years in the Valley, when conditions were still very raw and precarious, the Second General Epistle of the First Presidency imaged the land as "the valleys of Ephraim" and "the garden of Joseph." Indeed, they make it sound almost like the Garden of Eden when they declare, "The health of the Saints in the Valley is good, and it is so seldom that any one dies, we scarce recollect when such an event last occurred."[8]

How quickly certain images of Mormon country were impressed in people's imaginations is apparent in a rhapsodic oration delivered by young Leo Hawkins on the 24th of July, 1853:

Born among mobs and cradled on the billows of persecution, we have learned to appreciate the banquet of peace that we enjoy, in the valleys of Ephraim. Our cities arise in beauty and grandeur; our villages multiply; our fields teem with plenty; our flocks and herds abound; all nature seems to smile on us; in fact the wilderness and the solitary places have been made glad, and the desert has blossomed as a rose.[9]

No one imagined Mormon country more comprehensively than did Brigham Young, and no vision was more influential than his in shaping it. His discourses reveal that he envisioned a great commonwealth of Saints with neat, bustling cities and towns in which by a faithful adherence to the gospel and a care for the common good all members of society might prosper in righteousness. In one sermon, for example, he issued this challenge:

You count me out ten, fifty, a hundred, five hundred, or a thousand of the poorest men and women you can find in this community; with the means that I have in my possession, I will take these ten, fifty, hundred, five hundred, or a thousand people, and put them to labor; but only enough to benefit their health and to make their food and sleep sweet unto them, and in ten years I will make that community wealthy. . . . they shall be wealthy, shall ride in their carriages, have fine houses to live in, orchards to go to, flocks and herds and everything to make them comfortable.[10]

The reality never quite measured up to that vision, of course. Hence President Young's frequent irritation when he found on visiting a settlement how little had been accomplished since his last visit. Once, displeased that work was progressing so slowly on the Provo meeting-house, he threatened to move to Provo for a season, promising that he had "enough lightning" to make the work move along.[11] At times he must have wished he could divide himself into a hundred Brighams, each one to settle in a different valley and lead, coax, threaten, or inspire the inhabitants to make of their community what he envisioned it could become.

If Mormon country was the garden of Joseph, Brigham Young was the landscape architect and chief gardener. Garden imagery—as well as practical, down-to-earth advice about gardening—is very common in his discourses, and his regular "progresses" through the settlements were like the visits of a farmer to his various fields to see how the crops are maturing or whether the weeds are taking over. But it was no ordinary garden that he had in mind, as is clear from the instructions he gave to the Saints in Ogden in 1860 with one of the most striking images of human possibility that I know of: "Cultivate the earth," he said, "and cultivate your minds. Build cities, adorn your habitations, make gardens, orchards and vineyards, and render the earth so pleasant that when you look upon your labors you may do so with pleasure, and that angels may delight to come and visit your beautiful locations."[12] On that same trip in 1860, President Young explained to the people in Wellsville just what was to be the staple crop grown in the garden of Joseph. He said, "This is a splendid valley, and is better adapted to raising Saints than any other article that can be raised here. . . . It is the best country in the world for raising Saints."[13] Here perhaps is the origin and justification for the float that used to be a part of every Utah small-town Twenty-fourth of July parade: a wagon crammed full of children, with a sign on the side saying "Utah's Best Crop."

If the discourses of Brigham Young—and the many other general and local Church leaders—were crucial in shaping the image and meaning of Mormon country, the songs of Zion were a vital means of keeping these images present in people's minds. Except for "Come, Come, Ye Saints," which is actually a hymn of the trek, we seldom sing the regional hymns any more, but they used to be extremely popular, so that the people could dispense with song books and sing out with deep knowledge and feeling, "Our mountain home so dear,/ Where crystal waters clear/ Flow ever free." Or "Beautiful Zion for me/ Down in the valley reclining. . . . Clasped in the mountain's embrace,/ Safe from the spoiler forever. . . ." I can still hear the men's voices echoing through the long-since demolished meetinghouse in my Mormon village, as they roared out the refrain of "Ye Elders of Israel":

O Babylon, O Babylon, we bid thee farewell;
We're going to the mountains of Ephraim to dwell.

The hymn I alluded to in the title of my talk, "For the Strength of the Hills," is, interestingly enough, *not* Mormon in its origins. The text was written by Felicia Hemans, an English woman, and entitled "Hymn of the Vaudois Mountaineers in Times of Persecution." With its stirring image of mountain refuge, however, it was inevitable that it should be adopted by our people, especially with some added lines that evoke the Mormon persecutions:

At the hands of foul oppressors,
We've borne and suffered long;
Thou hast been our help in weakness,
And thy strength hath made us strong;
For the rock and for the river,
The valley's fertile sod;
For the strength of the hills we bless Thee,
Our God, our fathers' God.

If that song has a rival as the favorite song of Zion, it is Charles W. Penrose's "O Ye Mountains High." We can get some insight into the nature of image making when we realize that Elder Penrose had never seen Utah when he wrote this song. He was on a mission in England and had to frame his images of Mormon country from the rhetoric of Church messages and his own imagination of the appointed refuge. As a result the landscape description is quite conventional, but the sentiment struck an immediate chord in the Saints:

O ye mountains high, where the clear blue sky
Arches over the vales of the free,
Where the pure breezes blow and the clear streamlets flow,
How I've longed to your bosom to flee.

Indeed, this song, which at various times was entitled "Zion" and "Liberty," attained the status of a sort of patriotic hymn for the Saints, and it figured in a dramatic moment of Mormon history just two years after its publication. On 11 June 1858, during the "Utah War," as Edward Tullidge recounts the incident, the Church leaders were meeting with the federal peace commission while the invading army was supposedly camped in Echo Canyon. In the midst of the meeting, Porter Rockwell strode into the room with the report that the army was marching toward the city. The meeting immediately broke up in confusion, and Brigham Young said, "Is Brother Dunbar present? Brother Dunbar, sing 'Zion.'" And Brother Dunbar sang, no doubt to the discomfort of the peace commissioners, the militant original words of the song:

In thy mountain retreat, God will strengthen thy feet;
On the necks of thy foes thou shalt tread. . . .[14]

What the Saints created in their mountain retreat was a distinctive landscape, townscape, and way of life, the result of a unique combination of natural conditions and conscious design. They did not quite build a city in a day, but they did fill the valleys of Ephraim remarkably rapidly. Salt Lake City very early became, as Charles Peterson puts it, a "gathered place," passing quickly through "the period of colonizing during which Mormon institutions were most distinctive." And "the hinterland, where the process of the call, the trek, and the establishment of the village repeated itself, became the bulwark of Mormonism in its most distinctive form."[15] Villages were established wherever there was a stream of water for irrigation and a decent patch of level ground. Some of the settlements failed, but most remain today, scattered up and down the valleys, bearing names that stir the imagination just in the repeating: Lehi, Nephi, Manti, Bountiful, Brigham City, Heber City, Joseph City, Parowan, Panguitch, Paragonah, Paris, Snowflake, Orderville, Harmony, Fairview, Spring City, Fountain Green.

The scarcity of water confined settlement to the oases where mountain streams or springs flowed into the valley, and the necessity of irrigation required that settlements be communities of a certain size, since the irrigation works were beyond the power of a single family to build and maintain. But these natural constraints were congenial to the Mormons, who had always preferred the social, religious, and educational advantages of the town to the isolation of the homestead. What is more, the cooperative effort required by irrigation was a natural application of the principles of consecration and stewardship that had been planted in the Mormon consciousness before the trek west. Thus, in some respects the natural conditions reinforced the theory of Latter-day Saint society: cooperation was a virtue, a way of life that made Saints; it was also a necessity if there was to be life at all in this dry region.

The necessity of intensive development of resources in a land of natural scarcity harmonized also with an ethic of development in the Mormons. Many people today are accustomed to think that only a wilderness ethic embodies a true love for the earth, that the natural ecological balance is sacred and anything that alters it is evil. But for the early Mormon pioneer, a true love for the earth was expressed in reclaiming the wilderness, making of it a garden, restoring in so far as possible the original Garden that preceded the wilderness. When Levi Edgar Young composed his tribute to the pioneers on the centennial in 1947, he chose as his epigraph a passage from the Zend-Avesta which well embodies the pioneer image of the earth:

O maker of the world, thou holy one!
Who is it that rejoices the earth with greatest joy?
And the spirit answered:
It is he who sows corn, grass and fruits;
who waters ground that is dry,
and drains ground that is wet.
He who sows corn, sows righteousness.[16]

This ethic of intensive development, without which Mormon country could not have existed, did have some unfortunate consequences, however—most obviously the overgrazing that destroyed the fragile grasslands throughout most of the region. The Mormons made some deserts as well as gardens.[17]

It is the garden, though, whose meaning I am concerned with here, the valley-oasis drawing its life from the strength of the hills. No one from outside Mormon country can ever know the full meaning of the simple phrase "up the canyon." Up the canyon is the source of water, timber, grazing lands. Up the canyon lies perpetual springtime during summer's heat, camping, picnicking, fishing, and the recurring test of manliness in the annual deer hunt. The canyon is even a massive air-conditioning system, pouring out upon the valley a cool river of air the instant the sun sets.

At the mouth of the canyon, surrounded by its rich patchwork quilt of cropland, lies the village, deeply shaded by its trees. The heart of the village is the public square, the central block containing the tabernacle, courthouse, school, social hall, tithing office, or whatever portion of these key structures the town possessed. In larger towns, the important public buildings might overflow the square to adjacent blocks; in the smaller villages there might be nothing more than meetinghouse and schoolhouse, with room left over for a public recreation ground. Near the square, but rarely on it, is the small business section, dominated by the co-op store with its characteristic all-seeing eye. Thus the major human needs—religious, educational, social, commercial—were all met in the core of the town, within easy walking distance of every house, easy hearing distance, too, of the village clock or the meetinghouse bell that regulated life before the coming of "radio time."

Compared to other settlement patterns, the Mormon village is at once compact and spacious. It is compact in that the people are gathered into a townsite usually a mile square or less instead of living on scattered homesteads "gentile fashion," as Apostle E. T. Benson put it.[18] But within the town the dominant feeling is spaciousness: wide streets, open vistas, solid houses set deep on big lots, surrounded with orchards and gardens and cow pastures, and everywhere the pleasant gurgling of water in the irrigation ditches, a sharp contrast to the narrow, winding streets and tiny lots and houses of the non-Mormon mining camps that sprang up in the region.

From the earliest times there have been attempts to capture the essential images of the Mormon village, by scholars and casual visitors, natives and expatriates. For example, Florence Merriam, a non-Mormon who spent a summer in the 1890s in an unnamed village along the Wasatch Front (most likely Farmington), focused on the sounds and vistas, the numerous children everywhere, the distinctive institutions of polygamy, and the village celebrations, such as the village trek to the cemetery on Decoration Day.

Here is a sample of her first impressions:

Many of the streets were lined with locust-trees, whose white blossoms in June filled the air with their delicious fragrance. Under the trees ran mountain brooks, falling in white cascades down the hilly streets. Picturesque low stone houses were set back in bushy yards, each house with its orchard beside it— delightful old overgrown orchards, in which the children played and calves grazed in the dappling sunlight.

Long houses with two or more front doors excited our whispered comment, though we learned afterward that a new front door did not always mean a new wife. Children were everywhere. Almost every house had its baby. The most attractive were the little maidens whose flaxen curls and blue eyes were half hidden with demure pink or blue Mormon sunbonnets.[19]

Not every visitor found the spaciousness of the Mormon village appealing, though. For some it seemed merely a formless sprawl. Consider this diary entry from a soldier in Johnston's Army in 1860:

April 4th. . . . March down to Provo showed ourselves to the Ladies, took charge of four Mormon prisoners and started for Camp Floyd. Provo extends over a large space of ground but the houses are very much scattered, there is no building in it worth looking at, and the only thing remarkable, is a large mud hole as you enter the town, a fashionable place of resort for all the gentlemen swine in the neighborhood.[20]

The vital, organic form of the village can only be appreciated fully by those who were immersed in it in childhood, who

built treehouses high in towering ash trees, or lurched
through the streets on top of a load of hay bound from the
field outside of town to the big weathered barn at the
center of the block, or rose before first light to do winter
chores and experienced the comfort of seeing the neighbors'
barnyard lights come on and hearing them talk to their
cows, or watched the careers of the pigeons that nested in
the straw-thatched sheds, or knew the workings of the
great Mormon hay derricks, "whose silhouettes," as Austin
Fife has written, "like the spirits of ancestors, still fall
across the farmyards of the living."[21] In one of Virginia
Sorensen's novels, a man who has left Mormon country
gropes for the images that sum up his feeling for the place:
"This place is the shaking of hands, he thought. Ridges at
sunset. The rushing of cold clear streams. Long fertile
valleys and shining shared water weaving through the
fields. White temples. Children singing."[22]

Certain images recur again and again in attempts to
catch the flavor of Mormon country. One of them is trees.
"What can atone for the absence of trees in a landscape?"
lamented Elizabeth Wood Kane on surveying a barren
vista in southern Utah in the early 1870s.[23] The Mormons,
who had come from wooded regions, quite agreed with her
sentiments and were great tree planters, making of their
settlements orchard-villages, grove-villages. They planted
trees of all kinds: fruit trees, mulberries, locusts, black
walnuts, native cottonwoods, and box elders. But the
landmark Mormon trees were the lombardy poplars,
whose tall straight rows lined the streets of the towns and
sometimes marked property divisions in the fields. It is not
altogether clear why the poplars were planted so exten-
sively. They are fast-growing trees, which must have been
part of their appeal, and easily propagated by cuttings.
They are a good windbreak tree when planted in dense
rows, as they commonly were. To some observers the
poplars have seemed symbolically fitting in the Mormon
landscape. Wallace Stegner, for example, sees "a reflection

of Mormon group life in the fact that the poplars were practically never planted singly, but always in groups, and that the groups took the form of straight lines and ranks." He suggests that perhaps "the straight, tall verticality of the Mormon trees appealed obscurely to the rigid sense of order of the settlers, and that a marching row of plumed poplars was symbolic, somehow, of the planter's walking with God and his solidarity with his neighbors."[24]

But probably the most fundamental image and symbol of Mormon country is the irrigation system. The landscape is defined by its ditchlines much as the English countryside is marked by its ancient hedgerows, and the society is equally marked by the institutions of the "water turn" and the "water master." The water master, as Virginia Sorensen has said, was "an official of great importance in a Utah town"—a representative of the communal values— and the water thief, the individual who puts his own needs above the needs of the community, was a threat to the whole social fabric. Mrs. Sorensen's "Where Nothing Is Long Ago" is the story of the killing of a water thief and its effect on a Mormon town.

"But why did he hit him like that?" Mother asked my father. "It's not like Brother Tolsen to strike anybody. Such a gentle man!"

"Twice he had turned Brother Tolsen's water off his fields in the night. *Twice!*" My father spoke with the patience of a man obliged to explain violence to a woman.[25]

Nearly every Mormon community has somewhere in its history some crime of violence over water rights. One such incident in Kanab gave rise to a folk ballad:

In Kanab they will always remember
This Twenty-fourth of July
For this year there's no celebration,
No band plays and no pennants fly

. . . .

For two of the town's best men are lying
In their coffins awaiting the earth. . . .[26]

Even aside from such human conflicts, however, the irrigation system itself provided plenty of challenge. Any native of Mormon country can share the feelings of the song written by Moses Gifford and sung to the tune of "Hard Times Come Again No More":

'Tis the song and the prayer of the people:
Ditches, ditches, break again no more;
Many times we have mended places
in which you broke before.
O, ditches break that way no more.[27]

On the other hand, no music is sweeter than the soft singing of water in an irrigation canal, nothing more refreshing than to plunge your head into a ditch in the hayfield and feel it wash away the salt and heat and chaff.

If the cooperative irrigation system was both a burden and a joy, the cooperative store was almost an unalloyed joy. The coming of the co-op stores to the small towns of Mormon country brought to an end one of the most painful effects of isolation, the unavailability of consumer goods. Now it was possible for the sisters of Randolph and Scipio to wear dresses of the same fabrics as the Salt Lake ladies wore to conference. At the co-op store it was possible to buy not only city fabrics and corsets and chamber pots, but also such vital items as Dr. Janes Worm Remedy, Dr. Shores and Shores Catarrh Remedy, and Dr. Williams Pink Pills for Pale People. As William R. Palmer recalled of the Cedar City Co-op, "We were set up to cure any affliction of the flesh from infancy to old age. The one and only limitation we recognized was 'the Lord's own appointed time,' which we never tried to transcend, but even here we were able to keep the people alive up to the last minute before their time ran out."[28] The co-op also carried such luxuries as canned oysters for the oyster suppers that were favorite activities of the young people.

Besides bringing manufactured goods to the villages, the co-op store served as a sort of "produce bank" for home goods where eggs, hams, butter, and cheese could be traded for their value in goods that could not be produced at home. Many a school child in those days tried to trade the hard-boiled egg from his lunch bucket for an egg's worth of candy at the co-op. Some co-ops also maintained their own sawmills and tanneries. Mr. Palmer reported that the shoemaker at the Cedar City Co-op made a style of boots called "straights," which could be worn on either foot. The theory was that if you alternated the boots every day they would last twice as long.[29]

For those who preferred city shoes to the work of the local shoemaker, the co-op store brought some of the temptations of worldliness, including the trial of modesty involved in trying on shoes.

We were never supposed to touch a lady's stockinged foot [Mr. Palmer recalled]. The lady unbuttoned her shoe, then we took hold of the heel and toe and gently drew it off. The male clerk then held the new shoe open while the lady forced her foot in. In this gallant and romantic way, she tried on shoes until she found the pair she wanted. . . . All the while her long skirts were drawn snugly over her shins so that not an inch of leg was exposed above the shoe tops.[30]

Time does not allow an exploration of the numerous distinctive folkways that were bred in the isolation of Mormon country. There were the Danish nicknames of Sanpete Valley—Little Big Chris, Shimy Soren, Lead Pencil Peterson, Mart Stompey, and so on[31] —and the inventive Mormon names that Don Marshall has exploited so delightfully in his stories—Thurza, JaeNell, Leola, Neldean, LuGene, Wyoma, Utahna, Uvada, Osmer, Verdee, Veloy, and so on.[32] And not only Mormon names are distinctive but also Mormon pronunciations. Wayne Booth has written a clever essay suggesting that the linguistic distance from American *Fark* to New York is far greater than the distance in miles.[33]

I have said little so far about the center place of

Mormon country, Salt Lake City, and some question has been raised as to whether the distinctive characteristics of the region are to be found there. Charles Peterson has suggested that Salt Lake "may well have become the least Mormon of all Mormon places."[34] It seems to me, though, that there is a Mormon village hiding beneath the surface in Salt Lake City, if one knows where to look. Compared to other cities, Salt Lake has the same combination of compactness and spaciousness that the Mormon village displays when compared to other towns. It also maintains, like the Mormon village, an intimate relationship with its canyons, and in the heart of the city it is possible to come unexpectedly upon the sound of irrigation water gurgling in the ditch. Wallace Stegner has tried to find the right images for this distinctive urban ruralness in his most recent novel:

He has come to a place where Thirteenth East crosses the gully. The land falls away on the lower side into an unbuilt darkness that rattles with moving cottonwood trees. . . . Listen to those cottonwoods talking, he says to the two he left behind on the dark lawn. Doesn't that sound tell you, as much as any single signal in your life, who you are? Doesn't it smell of sage and rabbit brush and shad scale? Doesn't it have the feel of wet red ditch-bank sand in it, and the stir of a thunderstorm coming up over one of the little Mormon towns down in the plateaus? . . . When cottonwoods have been rattling at you all through your childhood, they mean *home*. . . . One puff wind through those trees in the gully is enough to tell me, not that I have come home, but that I never left.[35]

But the traces of Mormon country are occasional and fragmentary in Salt Lake City and so to an increasing extent are they throughout the region. St. George still has its beautiful tabernacle and temple and its red hills of November, but it is fast losing its traditional character and becoming, in the revealing Chamber-of-Commerce phrase, "the *other* Palm Springs." In my home town nearly all the barns are gone from the middle of the blocks, their places taken by trailer courts. And even those villages where the traditional patterns can still be seen almost intact—Spring City and Scipio, for example—are developing a self-consciousness that threatens to make them museum pieces rather than living communities.

So the regional period is over in Mormon country now. Actually, the Mormon village had a rather short prime. There were typically ten or fifteen years of hard pioneering, followed by a twenty- or thirty-year golden age when the fine houses and public buildings were constructed. By the end of that time the village had usually reached the limits that its watered land could maintain, and the majority of its young people were forced to go elsewhere to establish their own homes—elsewhere being the larger towns and cities in Mormon country or else outside the region altogether. As depopulation set in, so did a general decline; the trees matured and began to die, and few new ones were planted; smaller farms were absorbed into larger ones, and abandoned houses and barns were left to sag and eventually to fall, while the lilacs and yellow roses ran wild in the front yard. Eventually, what was left was a decaying world held together with baling wire, as we used to say, with widespread unemployment and neglect, apparent in the "whittle and spit gangs" that spent their days in idleness around the square. This decay produced a rich lore of its own, of course, such as the story of a visitor to Escalante who was appalled to see the weed-grown roadsides, the broken fences, and the generally run-down condition of things. At last, coming upon the "whittle and spit" gang leaning against a sunny wall, his irritation broke out: "Don't you fellows have anything better to do?" he demanded. "Mister," said one of the whittlers mildly, "we don't even *have* to do this if we don't want to."

Actually, most Mormon villages are less run-down today than they were thirty years ago, but the process of cleaning up has been largely a process of destruction of the distinctive elements.

So, once again, the age is over. But what does it mean?—since meaning is something we look for in the passing of an era. The answer to that question depends on how the images are read, and is often very personal. Lowry Nelson claimed that the Mormon village was a unique social invention, designed to usher in the Second Coming.[36] If that is the meaning, it seems to have failed. Charles Peterson has suggested that the Mormon village was a more or less deliberate strategy on Brigham Young's part to disperse the Saints so widely that it would take several generations for the world to find them.[37] If that was the strategy, it seems to have worked. By the strength of the hills, Mormon country was preserved as a sort of brood ground where large numbers of children were reared with a strong sense of Mormon identity, and then, because there was no way to maintain them at home, were sent out into the world where they formed the nucleus of new Latter-day Saint populations in many parts of the country. Perhaps the old-timers were right about Utah's best crop.

Finally, though, the meaning is individual and personal, as meanings always are. Eliot Butler has recalled coming home to Snowflake, Arizona, from his mission in a green land and finding the Snowflake country extremely barren. He asked his father why he remained there, and his father replied to the effect that he rather liked to live among people who could live in such a place. There is a meaning in that, I think. There is a meaning, too, in the summing up of an old farmer who was starved out after a struggle to establish a settlement on the Muddy River. According to Melvin Smith, the old man demanded, "Now what did we get out of that?" Then, reflecting a moment, he answered his own question: "Well, I guess we got experience."[38]

In the last analysis, what more than that do we get, though we dwell in marble halls?

Notes

In preparing this essay, I am aware of a far-reaching indebtedness to other scholars and imaginers of Mormon country. In addition to the specific citations that follow, I feel that I must acknowledge the influence of Thomas G. Alexander, Lavina Fielding Anderson, Leonard J. Arrington, Maureen Ursenbach Beecher, Davis Bitton, Juanita Brooks, Eugene Campbell, Eugene England, Joel E. Ricks, A. N. Sorensen, Samuel W. Taylor, Douglas H. Thayer, Woodruff C. Thomson, Maurine Whipple, and William A. Wilson.

1. Melvin T. Smith, "Forces That Shaped Utah's Dixie: Another Look," *Utah Historical Quarterly* 47 (1979): 112.

2. George Hicks, "Once I Lived in Cottonwood," *Mormon Songs from the Rocky Mountains: A Compilation of Mormon Folksong,* ed. Thomas E. Cheney (Austin: University of Texas Press, 1968), pp. 118-20.

3. Joseph Smith, *History of the Church of Jesus Christ of Latter-day Saints,* ed. B. H. Roberts, 6 vols. (Salt Lake City: Deseret News, 1902), 5: 85.

4. Ibid., 6:222.

5. Isaiah 2:2.

6. Quoted in Elizabeth Wood Kane, *Twelve Mormon Homes, Visited in Succession on a Journey Through Utah to Arizona* (Philadelphia, 1874), p. 96.

7. Quoted in William Mulder and A. Russell Mortensen, *Among the Mormons: Historic Accounts by Contemporary Observers* (New York: Alfred A. Knopf, 1958), p. 226. Richard H. Jackson has demonstrated the prevailingly favorable views of the early companies in his dissertation, "Myth and Reality: Environmental Perceptions of the Mormons, 1840-65, An Historical Geosophy" (Clark University, 1970), and in "Myth and Reality: Environmental Perception of the Mormon Pioneers," *Rocky Mountain Social Science Journal,* 9 (1972): 33-38.

8. Mulder and Mortensen, *Among the Mormons*, pp. 229, 232.

9. Quoted in Preston Nibley, *Brigham Young: The Man and His Work*, 4th ed. (Salt Lake City: Deseret Book Co., 1960), pp. 223-24.

10. Brigham Young, Address in the Tabernacle, Salt Lake City, 9 April 1871. In Brigham Young et al., *Journal of Discourses*, 26 vols. (Liverpool: Richards, et. al, 1854-87), 26: 175.

11. Brigham Young, Address in the Bowery, Provo, Utah, 14 July 1855, in *Journal of Discourses*, 3: 267.

12. Brigham Young, Address in Ogden, 12 June 1860, in *Journal of Discourses*, 8: 83.

13. Brigham Young, Address in Wellsville, Utah, 7 June 1860, in *Journal of Discourses*, 8: 288.

14. George D. Pyper, *Stories of Latter-day Saint Hymns* (Salt Lake City: Deseret News Press, 1939), p. 16.

15. Charles S. Petserson, *Utah: A Bicentennial History* (New York: W. W. Norton, 1977), p. 41.

16. Levi Edgar Young, "Spirit of the Pioneers," *Utah Historical Quarterly* 14 (1946): 5.

17. For a poignant account of this destruction, see Glynn Bennion, "A Pioneer Cattle Venture of the Bennion Family," *Utah Historical Quarterly* 34 (1966): 315-25.

18. Quoted in Peterson, *Utah*, p. 40.

19. Florence A. Merriam, *My Summer in a Mormon Village* (Boston and New York: Houghton, Mifflin, 1894), pp. 3-4.

20. "Charles A. Scott's Diary of the Utah Expedition, 1857-61," ed. Robert E. Stowers and John M. Ellis, *Utah Historical Quarterly* 28 (1960): 394.

21. Austin and Alta Fife, *Saints of Sage and Saddle: Folklore Among the Mormons* (Bloomington: Indiana University Press, 1966), p. 261.

22. Virginia Sorenson, *On This Star* (New York: Reynal and Hitchcock, 1946), p. 26.

23. Kane, *Twelve Mormon Homes*, p. 68.

24. Wallace Stegner, *Mormon Country* (New York: Duell, Sloan and Pearce, 1942), pp. 23-24.

25. Virginia Sorensen, *Where Nothing Is Long Ago: Memories of a Mormon Childhood* (New York: Harcourt, Brace and World, 1963), pp. 7-8.

26. Olive W. Burt, *American Murder Ballads*, quoted in Cheney, *Mormon Songs*, pp. 193-95.

27. Cheney, *Mormon Songs*, pp. 153-54.

28. William R. Palmer, "Early Merchandising in Utah," *Utah Historical Quarterly* 31 (1963): 42-43.

29. Ibid., p. 48.

30. Ibid., pp. 47-48.

31. James Boyd Christensen, "Function and Fun in Utah Danish Nicknames," *Utah Historical Quarterly* 39 (1971): 24-30.

32. All of these names, and several more, are found in a single story by Don Marshall, "The Reunion," *Frost in the Orchard* (Provo, Utah: Brigham Young University Press, 1977), pp. 156-67.

33. Wayne C. Booth, "Farkism and Hyperyorkism," *Now Don't Try to Reason with Me: Essays and Ironies for a Credulous Age* (Chicago: University of Chicago Press, 1970), pp. 267-71.

34. Peterson, *Utah*, p. 41.

35. Wallace Stegner, *Recapitulation* (Garden City, N.Y.: Doubleday, 1979), pp. 114, 116.

36. Lowry Nelson, *The Mormon Village: A Pattern and Technique of Land Settlement* (Salt Lake City: University of Utah Press, 1952), p. 28.

37. Charles Peterson, "A Mormon Town: One Man's West," *Journal of Mormon History* 3 (1976): 10-12.

38. Melvin T. Smith, "Forces That Shaped Utah's Dixie," p. 129.

4

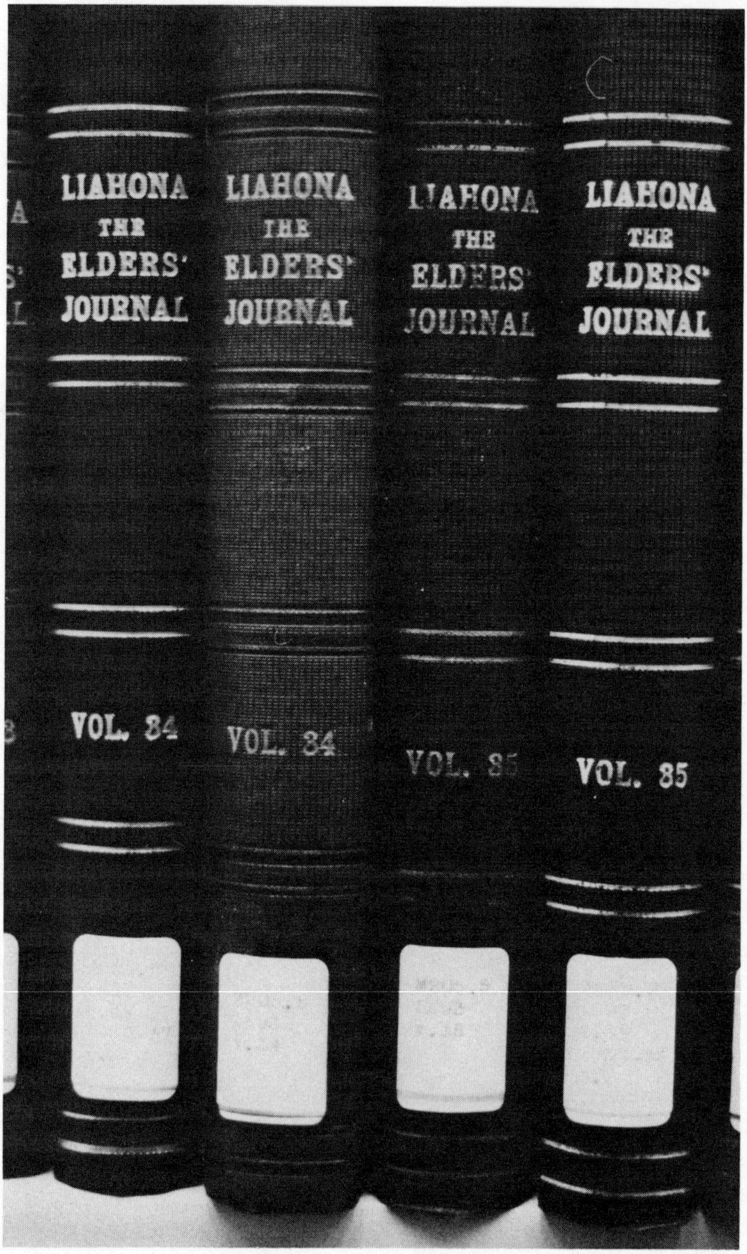

The Dawning of a Brighter Day: Mormon Literature After 150 Years

Eugene England

It is interesting to contrast the generally optimistic tone of the following essay by Eugene England, Associate Professor of English at Brigham Young University, and the generally pessimistic essay by Emma Lou Thayne in The Mormon People: Their Character and Traditions, *number ten of the Redd Monograph series. One would hardly believe that they are dealing with the same literary tradition.*

Nevertheless, it is possible to reconcile the two points of view when one realizes that they are really not writing about the same aspect of Mormon literature. Professor Thayne is critiquing the literature printed recently in official church publications. Professor England has in mind a literary tradition, found today principally among Mormon academics and in independent journals and books, that is seriously concerned with producing a literary genre which can rank with the best in American fiction and poetry and which is nevertheless infused with a sense of deep understanding of and commitment to the Latter-day Saint community and beliefs.

Beyond his prescription for the elements necessary to produce such literature, Professor England has provided a useful analysis of Mormon literary history. He sees the development of Mormon literature as passing through four stages. The first generation (1830-1880) included the writings of the founders and their immediate successors. The middle or fallow period (1880-1930) produced essentially home literature and some rather poor novels, and was most noted for its theological and historical writing. The second or lost generation (1930-1960) can be characterized by some fine novels often produced by somewhat disaffected Latter-day Saints. Finally, the third generation (1960 to the present) consists of a group of essayists, novelists, and poets following on the heels of Clinton Larson's work.

We find the logic of the following essay compelling and are convinced that Professor England is right in believing that Latter-day Saints stand on the verge of some important breakthroughs in an increasingly vigorous literary tradition.

In the first essay of this volume, Jan Shipps did a remarkable thing. She analyzed, sympathetically, a period of apparent great change in Mormon history. This in itself is no longer unusual, even for a non-Mormon like Professor Shipps, but she began her study with a new assumption for non-Mormon historians—that Mormonism is a genuine *religious* movement, like other genuine and respected religious movements. That assumption yielded important results for her as a historian, accurate perceptions about how fundamental religious experiences and a fundamental mythic vision do persist, despite the dramatic surface changes in Mormon cultural and institutional forms. And that assumption also has implications for Mormon literature.

Here I ask you to consider, on the basis of what I believe is adequate evidence, the following: Mormonism is a genuine religious movement, with persistent and characteristic religious and cultural experiences growing out of a unique and coherent theology and a powerful mythic vision, and it has already produced and is producing the kinds and quality of literature that such experiences and vision might be expected to produce. It is, in fact, right now enjoying a kind of bright dawning, a flowering, in its literary history.

Many of us, at least until recently, could be excused for not knowing there is a Mormon literature. A serious anthology of Mormon literature, providing a full view of the quality and variety over the Church's nearly 150-year history, was first published only a few years ago. That was

Richard Cracroft and Neal Lambert's *A Believing People.*[1] At about the same time, those two scholars inaugurated, at Brigham Young University, the first course in Mormon literature. The Association for Mormon Letters, the first professional organization intended to study and encourage Mormon literature, is only five years old. There is as yet no scholarly bibliography of Mormon literature, no full-scale literary history or developed esthetic principles, little practical and less theoretical literary criticism. The most basic scholarly work—the unearthing and editing of texts, development of biographical materials, and serious literary analysis of acknowledged classics—is still largely undone. In fact, the study of Mormon history, in terms of maturity and respectability in its own scholarly community, is a good ten years ahead of Mormon literature, largely because of the leadership of people like Thomas Alexander, Leonard Arrington, James Allen, Richard Anderson, and others from BYU and elsewhere. It makes sense that similar leadership in Mormon literature, both its creation and criticism, should now begin to develop. Indeed, there are probably many who will read this essay who are not only already contributors to Mormon literature but who will be encouraged to help with the flowering—the brighter day—I anticipate. But though my aim is high, my hopes are necessarily modest. I am casting myself out into a vast and marshy area where few footholds have been established— into esthetics, into criticism of unusual forms and of very recent work. I could well have used the honored French tradition in my title: something like "Notes Toward a Mormon Esthetic and a Mormon Literary History," something to remind you how tentative, though serious, all this is. Perhaps it is too much to even hope to blaze a trail.

But then again, to look more optimistically, many things *are* happening, and perhaps there is now less excuse for any continued ignorance or inaction. The anthology had a second printing, the Mormon literature class continues to prosper, and Mormon classics are being used in other literature and humanities courses. Two fine new journals, *Exponent II* and *Sunstone*, are succeeding and are following the older Dialogue's tradition of publishing good Mormon literature and criticism, and official Church magazines like the *Ensign* are publishing more real literature than they previously have. We have recently seen the publication and widespread approval of the biography of Spencer W. Kimball, the first Mormon study of a general Church leader that meets the essential criterion for genuine literary biography (identified by Virginia Woolf as "those truths which transmit personality"). Others are in the works that may do the same for past Church presidents.

In just the last two years much has developed, almost in a crescendo. The Association of Mormon Letters met at BYU and evidenced signs of maturity and growing vitality as important ground-breaking essays on the Book of Mormon as literature and on classics of Mormon fiction were presented. Three books by established Mormon poets (Clinton Larson, Ed Hart, and Marden Clark) have been published, and some impressive younger poetic voices have appeared in the journals.[2] We even have a Mormon epic poem—by Paul Cracroft.[3] Douglas Thayer has expanded his range to an experimental novel dealing with the development of consciousness of evil and redemption in a young Mormon. Bruce Jorgensen has written a well-crafted, mature story on baptism and initiation that is fine literature, not merely Mormon.[4] Bela Petsco has published a collection of stories centered in missionary experience.[5] Last fall we saw the small body of serious Mormon drama augmented by performances here of Thomas Rogers's *Reunion*, a study of classic Mormon conflicts. And just in the last few months Ed Geary, working to stretch and develop the genre I think most congenial to the Mormon vision and experience, the personal essay, has made good on his earlier promise, pulled back from what many of us worried was a surrender to Mammon in the form of the *Deseret News*, where his entertaining but rather formulary reminiscences have been appearing, and has proven that he was merely in training to produce another knockout like "Goodbye to Poplarhaven."[6] And he has done so, with an even better exploration of Mormon consciousness called "Hying to Kolob," that is fine literature accessible to all.[7] So my hope is high: "The morning breaks."

But, you may rightly be saying, one, or even three, bursting forsythia do not make a spring—nor a Larson and a Thayer and a Geary a flowering of literature, Mormon or not. And others of you might well ask, "What is this 'Mormon' literature anyway—something like 'Lutheran' literature or 'Christian Science' literature?" If you have been exposed to some of the agonizing that has been going on for some twenty years about Mormons not having an obviously impressive literature, you might ask, "Aren't we too young a culture or too small a community to expect to have a literature—or aren't Mormons too superficially happy, too anxiety- and conflict-free, to produce a literature, or too busy, or too smug, or too anti-intellectual, or too materialistic, or too censored?" The answer to all these questions is "No." Because there is in fact a Mormon literature—one whose shape, dimensions, and quality are becoming more and more apparent and impressive. These questions and anxieties are now simply outdated; reality has long passed them by, and good theoretical thinking has caught up with them. The real question now is not how good is what we have, but how is it good?. How, in fact, do we judge how it is good? And how do we prepare better to respond to it and to encourage more of the good?

But some may still be saying, "Suppose we do have some good writers. Why talk about Mormon literature rather than American literature, or better yet, just literature? Shouldn't our writers just do their best, write honestly and well about the universal human concerns, and address themselves to mankind in general?" Perhaps, but let me suggest another case: Shakespeare and Milton had access to audiences, a *literate* community, smaller than that which is now made up of well-educated English-speaking Mormons (which is approaching three million). Does it in any way count against those great poets that they spoke directly and consciously to that limited audience from a base in particular problems, perspectives, and convictions that were essentially English? Or does it count against Dostoevski that he was consciously, even self-consciously, Russian, or Faulkner that he was consciously Southern?

The only way to the universal is through the particular. The only honesty ultimately is honesty to that which we know in our own bones and blood and spirit, our own land and faith, our own doubts and battles and victories and defeats. Mormonism cannot be separated from these things because, unlike religions such as Lutheranism or Christian Science, it makes a large number of intractable, ultimate claims about the nature of the universe and God and human beings, about specific historical events, past and future, about language and form and content—and because it is grounded in a sufficiently unusual and cohesive and extended historical and cultural experience growing directly from those claims that it has become like a nation, an ethnic culture as well as a religion. We can speak of a Mormon literature at least as surely as we can of a Jewish or Southern literature. And it is as legitimate, as promising, for a writer to be consciously Mormon as it has been for Flannery O'Connor to be Southern Catholic or for Isaac Bashevis Singer to be emigré Polish and Jewish.

Mormon writers have much to learn from both of these writers: skills and vision, of course, but also how not to be so universal they lose contact with their roots, so antiparochial they adopt the worst kind of parochialism— that of not knowing oneself and one's own generic community. They can learn from them how to translate religious commitment and the tragedy of religious struggle and paradox into honesty and craft, into fictive creations rather than packaged preachments. As Flannery O'Connor has said:

I see from the standpoint of Christian orthodoxy. This means that for me the meaning of life is centered in our Redemption by Christ and what I see in the world I see in its relation to that. I don't think that this is a position that can be taken halfway or one that is particularly easy in these times to make transparent in fiction.[8]

But of course her special Catholic vision, however effectively pointing beyond itself to the universal, cannot be adopted by the Mormon writer. The Mormon vision has unique and equally powerful implications for both form and content. What are they? Just what is a *Mormon* literature?

First, it is obviously literature written by and about Mormons. And that definition has served well in the early stages of exploration. But it has not helped much in developing literary theory and stimulating better literature, and it opens up controversies about certain fringe areas concerning which already too much ink has been spilt. What about Wallace Stegner's *Mormon Country* (a non-Mormon writing about Mormons)? Or, on the other hand, what about May Swenson, who was indubitably raised a Mormon but whose connection with Mormon perspectives, in either the content or form of her poetry is, I must confess, nearly imperceptible to me. Too bad, because Swenson and Stegner are internationally prestigious writers. And that, I fear, is why we want to claim them. There is that old Mormon hunger to be well spoken of, to enjoy prestigious connections. It's time to cast off such psychological crutches, which are now I think essentially distracting, and become more specific, even prescriptive, in our definitions. Let me propose some starting places, some footholds in the bog that might eventually be built up to make a road.

I think Karl Keller is right in suggesting that Mormon

writers—possibly due to that parochial antiparochialism I mentioned and an understandable aversion to didactic, simplistically preachy Mormon writing—have produced fiction that is by and large irrelevant to the doctrinal interests of Mormonism. He calls most of what we've written "jack-fiction."[9] In contrast with Flannery O'Connor, many Mormon writers seem to have strained, in the fashion of various schools of emancipated realism, to be far from orthodoxy. Even the "orthodox" have not written imaginative visions of the possibilities of our theology; it is not really *Mormon* fiction. By way of contrast, this is O'Connor on what was important to her that she work out imaginatively in her fiction:

It makes a great difference to the look of a novel whether its author believes that the world came late into being and continues to come by a creative act of God, or whether he believes that the world and ourselves are the product of a cosmic accident. It makes a great difference to his novel whether he believes that we are created in God's image, or whether he believes we create God in our own. It makes a great difference whether he believes that our wills are free, or bound like those of the other animals.[10]

Surely we could make an equally specific list for a Mormon writer. But neither O'Connor nor Keller are suggesting some sophisticated form of packaged message. Any artist's first responsibility is to the form, the embodiment, the word made flesh. If he or she cannot do justice to the visible world and make of it fictions that are believable, he cannot be trusted to bear witness to the invisible world; like Flannery O'Connor, Mormon writers must see and imagine steadily and whole—in convincing formal structures—the surface, including oppositions and evil, the terror in natural human experience, before they can see and imagine how the supernatural supports or intrudes upon that surface.

But if Keller is right, we may have a major explanation

for the unfulfilled promise of Mormon fiction. It has effectively imagined the Mormon past and some of the conflicts inherent in contemporary Mormon public and private life but has left Mormonism's unique God and the dramatic and unusual Mormon view of man's cosmic dilemma and destiny out of the picture. The fact that some are making a beginning in those new directions is a major reason I expect the dawning of a brighter day.

Let me try to be more specific. Though definitions tend to be limiting, my *intention* at least is to expand our awareness of fruitful possibilities. And though it is ultimately impossible to separate form and content, and dangerous to try, let me begin with a few comments on form. In the "King Follett Discourse," itself a classic piece of Mormon literature, Joseph Smith refers to "chaotic matter—which is element and in which dwells all the glory."[11] That helps bring into imaginative focus the hints throughout scripture and the writings of Mormon thinkers that suggest a certain metaphysics of form; order is wrought from a pluralistic chaos but a chaos that is potent, genuinely responsive to the creative powers of God and man embodied in mind and language, characteristics God and his children share as literally related beings. The Doctrine and Covenants (88:6-11) ties together the divine mind and cosmic creative power of Christ with man's perception through the media of physical and spiritual light, which are pronounced to be fundamentally the same. All this suggests the seeds of a philosophy of form at least as interesting and defensible as epistemological skepticism— the debased philosophical idealism called nominalism— that has contributed to the breakdown in structure characteristic of modern literature. A truly Mormon literature would stand firm against secular man's increasing skepticism about the efficacy of language to get at the irreducible otherness of things outside the mind—to make sense, and beauty, of that "chaotic matter—which is element." The ultimate implication of such skepticism (as

George Steiner and other critics have reminded us and Melville *showed* us in his novel *Pierre, or the Ambiguities* and in his life) is absolute silence, which is hardly a solution for human beings, especially writers. And so the nature and degree of their *compromises* with their skepticism is what constitute modern writers' various styles.

But if Mormon writers take seriously the fact that language is a gift from God, the creator, that gives them access to the "glory" that dwells in matter and in other intelligences, including God's, they can confidently use language, not like others merely to imitate (albeit with compassionate despair) the separated, meaningless, raw elements and experiences of a doomed universe, but to create genuinely new things, verbal structures of element and intelligence and experience that include understanding and judgment as well as imitation and empathy. We can, like our contemporaries, create of words what Wallace Stevens called "things that do not exist without the words," but we can do so without his undermining fear that what he was doing was merely an ephemeral human activity, a game to occupy until final doom; we can be sustained by the faith that what we are doing is rooted ontologically and shared by God.

In other words there should be in Mormon writers a special respect for language and form, attention to its tragic limitations but also to its real possibilities. This would mean, I would think, a rather conservative respect for proven traditional forms until they are genuinely understood and surpassed. At least it would mean unusual resistance to the flight from form, from faith in language, toward obscurity and proud assertion of the purely personal vision that afflicts so much writing in our time.

Now what about content? Obviously, Mormon literature will draw, as much of it already has, on certain specially evocative characteristics of Mormon history and scriptural narrative. I do not mean irrigation and polygamy and Lamanite warriors but rather a certain epic consciousness and mythic identification with ancient peoples and processes: the theme of exile and return, of the fruitful journey into the wilderness; the pilgrim traveling the dark and misty way to the tree of salvation; the lonely quest for selfhood that leads to conversion and then to the paradox of community; the desert as crucible in which to make saints, not gold; the sacramental life that persists in spiritual experience and guileless charity despite physical and cultural deprivation; the fortunate fall from innocence and comfort into a lone and dreary world where opposition and tragic struggle can produce virtue and salvation. Much remains to be done with these. And it would be *Mormon* literature—though, of course, not exclusively so, since we share forms of these mythic truths with various others.

Then there are certain contemporary concomitants of our underlying cultural heritage and beliefs that provide unusually rich, though again not unique, dramatic possibilities: for instance, both the unusual sense of order and also the openings to tragic failure provided a life by the making of covenants, of promises to self and God in baptism and weekly communion through bread and water; or the fearful, solemn, and nobly exciting dimension given marriage by promises of obedience and fidelity and consecration made before God and angels on holy ground. What can be done with a physical and mental landscape peopled perhaps even more literally than Isaac Singer's with devils, with embodiments of ultimate, intransigent evil who mock and betray, and also peopled with translated beings—ancient Nephites—who bemuse folklorists and bless simple folk from Panguitch and Downey, with angels who bring glad tidings to wise and holy men, and to women and children who are thus inspired to speak great and marvelous, unspeakable things? And what can be done with the Mormon animism that hears the earth groan with its wickedness or the mountains shout for joy, that moves people to bless oxen and crops, even automobiles and trees? What can be made of the spiritual literalness that

hears a daughter calling for help on the other side of the
world or takes in stride faithfulness that is stronger than
the cords of death and brings dead friends and family on
privileged visits back to comfort and instruct? Fine non-
Mormon poets, W. S. Merwin for one, have written
beautifully of the deep yearning we have for the miracle of
a dead loved one's return to us—and of the strange
possibility.[12] Mormons with a more literal belief have the
resources to do as well and better, if they have the courage
of their convictions and the discipline to work as hard to
create an honest visible world that the invisible world can
break through. And it is because for Mormons, as for
Gerard Manley Hopkins, "the Holy Ghost over the bent/
World broods with warm breast and with ah! bright
wings."

John Fowles, in his novel *Daniel Martin*, speaks of
feeling "like an empiricist threatened with supernatural
pattern." What a fine theme, especially available for
balanced use by Mormons who have been hushed and
thrilled in the presence of supernatural patterns but can
still empathize with the empiricism, the doubt, in all of us,
a theme even more available, perhaps, than to an empiricist
who *will* not even be threatened.

But there is even a deeper layer, as yet hardly touched
in Mormon literature but with, I believe, the greatest
potential for uniqueness and power, the one suggested
directly by Flannery O'Connor's list. It would require more
theological literacy and more imaginative response to our
theology. Karl Keller, in the essay mentioned earlier,
suggests that Mormon writers should begin with careful
reading of Sterling McMurrin's *The Theological Foundations of
the Mormon Religion*, which he calls "essentially an outline of
the esthetic possibilities of Mormon articles of belief." I
would add Joseph Smith and B. H. Roberts, and John
Widtsoe and Hugh B. Brown and Truman Madsen and,
yes, Brigham Young and Joseph Fielding Smith and Spencer
W. Kimball and the Doctrine and Covenants and Pearl of

Great Price— and, from the Book of Mormon, II Nephi 2 and Alma 42, and so forth. And what could that do for a Mormon writer, other than tempt him toward a suicidal didacticism? It could nurture his imagination with the most challenging and liberating set of metaphysical possibilities and paradoxes I have been able to discover in all human thought. Consider only a few, beginning with the keystone: that human beings, like the gods, are at core uncreated and underived, individual intelligences, without beginning or end; they are possessed of truly infinite potential, literal gods in embryo, but are bound inescapably in a real environment of spirit and element and other beings that impinge upon them and that, as they learn successfully to relate to the environment, exact real costs in suffering and loss and bring real joy in relationship and growth.

Freedom, for a Mormon writer—or fictional character— is not a mysterious illusion, as it must be for traditional Christians with their absolute, omnipotent God, nor is it a pragmatic tautology, as it must be for existentialists who define existence, however temporary, as freedom. Freedom is ultimate and inescapable responsibility in a real world that is neither a shadow of something more real lying beyond it that God determines at will nor a doomed accident. The consequences for dramatic action and lyric reflection seem to be considerable. For one thing, as Truman Madsen has said, "Suicide is just a change of scenery." For another, as the amateur Mormon theologian B. F. Cummings put it, "The Self is insubordinate, wandering, imperially aloof, solitary, lonely, withdrawn, unvisited, impenetrable"; it "cannot escape from existence nor can it escape from the awareness of its existence" nor from the "inevitable sense of solitude" that is "born of the very fact of individuality," of "being an eternally identical one."[13] Put that together with the equally firm teaching that man without God is nothing, less than the dust of the earth (for the elements are at least obedient to God's creative will), that mortals are utterly dependent upon God, who sustains, moment by moment, their existence in mortality though not their eternal essence, and who provides the only way of salvation through relation to his Son. And put it together with that strange paradox of the Atonement, the fortunate fall: each individual *must* lose innocence, experience opposition and sin, know failure, struggle with justice and guilt, before he or she will let Christ break the bonds of justice, tear down the barriers within to bring the bowels of mercy—and so accept himself in love and thus have strength to develop the conscious, intelligent virtues of Christ. And put all this together with the idea that, imperially alone and impenetrable as the individual is, he and she cannot fully and ultimately realize their own true nature and achieve their fullest potential and joy except in the ongoing struggle of an eternal, fully sexual, companionship—an idea authenticated by the Mormon image of God as being God precisely and only in such a female and male companionship.

But I indicated I would actually try to come down to a list of specific ideas by which to define a special literature. A Mormon literature, it seems to me, would imaginatively evoke O'Connor's Christian "differences" as she calls them: a world created and continually brought into new being by God rather than a cosmic accident; a God in whose image we are created rather than one we create in ours; and a will that is uniquely free rather than bound like that of other animals. We would then add such things as these, as special differences, beyond the general Christian ones: An open, infinitely possible universe that calls to optimistic adventure because it is full of things and beings that have always existed and will always exist, rather than a closed, ultimately mysterious universe called into being out of nothing and liable to capricious change or end at God's inscrutable will. A God whom we can trust absolutely because he has triumphed in the kind of environment and process we are experiencing and has gained all possible power and knowledge with regard to our salvation. But a God who also is a powerful encouragement to our dynamic thirst for infinitely continuing learning and righteous adventure because God has taught us that those processes continue for Him and Her together in spheres of existence that extend infinitely beyond even them—with companions and models we can only dream of. A sense of awe about oneself and every other mortal, grounded in awareness of their uncreated, indestructible core of being, containing, as a seed contains the oak, the potentiality of literal godhood. But an awe grounded also in respect for others' long premortal development as children of God and their courageous decision to enter into this perplexing and painful earth life, where their spirits are learning to coexist with matter and to live through the dramatic paradoxes of faith as a preparation for the adventures ahead. I could go on, but I mean to be only provocative—and already feel the danger of being misunderstood.

I am *not* proposing a formal creed for Mormon writers. Stephen Tanner, in a recent essay exploring the relationship of literature to moral and religious concerns, an important part of the groundwork for a Mormon literary criticism, has reminded us of the destructive effects of trying to write from a creed and also of the nature of the creative process, that that process responds to the complexity and indeterminacy of actual human experience rather than the logic of formal beliefs.[14] What an author is, of course, is more important than what he avowedly believes, and a literary work must be judged for what it actually is, not what it states. I am merely suggesting that there is available to Mormon writers, part of what they in fact already are, a rich loam—a topsoil of historical experience, mythic consciousness, and unique theology— as rich as that available to any other writers, more rich than that of most of their gentile contemporaries. To change the image to one that has characteristically been made into a Mormon cliché, I suggest we put down our

buckets where we are rather than complaining of thirst or
rowing so madly for foreign shores. Even if rooting
ourselves in that rich topsoil would tend to limit us to a
Mormon or traditional Christian audience—and I am not,
on the example of O'Connor and Singer ready to grant
that—but even so, that is a large enough and worthy
enough audience, and one that needs as much as any to be
served by the values that literature can provide. We in the
Mormon community need to be brought out of our
existential loneliness, to experience what other Mormons
feel, to understand imaginatively and share with each
other our fears and doubts—the joys and small victories in
the communal and individual working out of our salvation.
If the gospel is true in any essential sense, there need be no
greater ambition for Mormon literature—at least, to begin
with.

These suggestions I have made about a definition of
Mormon literature and about a Mormon esthetic are,
again, only preliminary, but even with this small beginning
we have, I think, enough on which to base some useful
outlines for a literary history. Let me suggest one scheme
based on this definition that may be helpful conceptually
and evocative of further study. One way of seeing our
literary history is in terms of three fifty-year periods and
three kinds of rebels. During the first fifty years or so—
into the 1880s—a uniquely Mormon, nontraditional literature was produced by men and women caught up in the
restored gospel's rebellion against the world, against
Babylon. For them it was literally and ecstatically true, as
one of their fine hymns expressed it, that "the morning
breaks, the shadows flee" and that "the glory bursting
from afar, wide o'er the nations soon will shine."[15] They
rejected, with powerful arguments, the economic, political
and moral conditions of England and Europe and America;
and with incredible courage and self-sacrifice they built
genuine alternatives that continue to thrill us. And, I

submit, they produced an extraordinary and valuable literature about their feelings, thoughts, and experiences, literature we have too long neglected but are beginning to recover and appreciate—to learn *how* to appreciate—as we should.

Many of us who study literature professionally have become increasingly uneasy in the past twenty years about the inadequacy of formalist criteria, that is, those concerned mainly with esthetic qualities—structure, style, organization, and so forth—the matters emphasized in the New Criticism that held sway in mid-twentieth century literary criticism. We have discovered their inadequacy to account for our experiences—and that of our students—with certain literature, such as that, for instance, called to our attention as ethnic or women's literature, some of which has powerfully affected us despite its apparent lack of great formal or esthetic qualities. We have been brought slowly to recognize that there are also, in good literature, important social and religious and moral values. These are sometimes bound inseparably with the formal perfections; they sometimes provide some compensation for lack of formal training or traditional stylistic ability; and sometimes they actually push naive or inexperienced writers toward formal qualities they did not consciously work for. For instance, in the powerful reminiscence of Mary Goble Pay,[16] the moving formal purity of understatement comes, I believe, from her own religious and moral qualities and the religious and moral extremity of the situation, not from any literary training or models, most of which would have been bad. Ironically, it has been mainly non-Mormon scholars who have done the most to help us deal with these new problems and possibilities, without neglecting formalist values. Critics like Yvor Winters, Ian Watt, Wayne Booth, Robert Scholes, E. D. Hirsch, and John Gardner have explored some of the neglected social, moral, and religious values in literature and the critical means for understanding and evaluating literature in terms of them.

If we are to properly evaluate, or even understand and appreciate, our Mormon literature, particularly in the first fifty years, we must build on their work.

The second fifty years, from about 1880 to 1930, is a barren period in Mormon literature, with, I believe, hardly anything of lasting value published or written (at least in the usual literary genres). But there are important literary as well as historical questions to be answered by a study of that period, questions about the nature of the Church after the disappointment of the popular expectation of Christ's coming in 1890, the Manifesto of that year (in the view of many a capitulation to the government and secular American society), and the period of accommodation to American styles and values that followed. Historians and literary critics need to work together to understand the relations between Church and culture in this difficult period. And one phenomenon they will need to look at carefully is that during this time there was an outpouring of poems, stories, and novels, mainly in the Church magazines and press, that were known as "home literature" and were designed for the edification of the Saints. At first look, many have assumed that such literature was so bad and so deadening an influence on Mormon literary culture in general because it was too Mormon; I believe it was not Mormon enough. Edward Geary is right in making a distinction that applies to that literature and from which we can learn some lessons that apply directly today, when we face the same dangers as well as the equally great danger of overreaction to those dangers. In his landmark essay on Mormon regional fiction, Geary notes that the home literature movement, which began in the 1880s, was an explicit instrument for spreading the gospel, one which, in Apostle and poet Orson Whitney's words "like all else with which we have to do, must be made subservient to the building up of Zion."[17] In explaining why that movement has not met Elder Whitney's hope that Mormonism would produce "Miltons and Shakespeares of our own," Geary writes:

> It is one thing to ask the artist to put his religious duties
> before his literary vocation or to write from his deepest
> convictions. It is quite another to insist that he create from a
> base in dogma rather than a base in experience. . . . [Home
> literature] is not a powerful literature artistically, nor is it
> pure. In most cases its distinctive Mormon characteristics are
> only skin deep, masking an underlying vision which is as
> foreign to the gospel as it is to real life.[18]

For example, think of the popular, entertaining, and
"edifying" *Saturday's Warrior*, with its slick sophistication,
its misleading if not heretical theology, and its stereotyping
toward bigotry in the social references—under the skin as
foreign to the gospel as to real life. Geary continues, "The
early home literature borrowed the techniques of popular
sentimental fiction and the values of the genteel tradition
with a superficial adaptation to Mormon themes, and this
practice continues only slightly modified."

You can easily see the continuing influence of that
movement in the official magazines and in Church press
novels of today; but it is perhaps at least as unfortunate
that the reaction against that movement, however well
intentioned, also too often fails to see the superior Mormon
literature available or the importance and possibility of
trying to produce it. We even, in our intemperate reaction,
sometimes forget Geary's distinction—that though it is
illegitimate and destructive to insist that a writer create
from dogma rather than experience, it might well be
legitimate and valuable to ask him, as I think the Church
properly does, to put his religious duties before his literary
vocation or to write from his deepest convictions.

After that long hiatus in the middle of Mormon
literature, we have had a period of about fifty years of
considerable output and much quality, but by two quite
different kinds of rebels from two *literary* generations that
overlap. The first of these began most prominently with

Vardis Fisher in the 1930s, and has lingered, in Samuel
Taylor, up into the early 1970s. It has been aptly characterized by Ed Geary as Mormondom's "lost generation."[19]
And Geary has shown that the writers were, like American
literature's "lost generation" of twenty years before,
defined by their various degrees of rebellion against their
"provincial" culture, by a patronizing alienation infused
with nostalgia for a vanishing way of life that would not let
them turn completely away to other loyalties and subject
matter, even when they became in one way or another
expatriated. They were the first generation of the twentieth century, growing up when Mormon isolation was
breaking down, rural Mormondom was depopulating, and
urban Mormonism was apparently becoming crassly
materialistic. It was easy for them to see the Church,
however heroic in the nineteenth century, as failing, the
Mormon experiment as rapidly ending. And they saw
themselves as the first well-educated generation of Mormonism, able to look with some amusement upon the
naiveté of Mormon thought.

Such rather adolescent alienation has persisted in
many intellectuals of that generation, some who were my
teachers in the 1950s at the University of Utah, for
instance. It has persisted despite the refutations provided
by historical reality and the more insightful historical
analysis that recently has been done (such as that of Jan
Shipps, for instance, which has identified the continuing
underlying vitality of Mormon faith) and despite the
achievements that were being made even *during* that period
in such areas as well-written theology and history, by B. H.
Roberts, John A. Widtsoe, and others. The "lost generation"
of writers, and those who shared their sense of Mormonism's decline, actually thought there would not be
another generation after them. And as late as 1969 Dale
Morgan, writing on Mormon literature, could say, "A lot
of the urgency has gone out of [the Mormon] sense of
mission as the millennial expectation has subsided and the

powerful 'gathering' phase of Mormon history has run its course."[20] That was written just before the remarkable new missionary energies, the growth to genuine world status and millennial vision, that have come in the 1970s. As Geary writes, "From the viewpoint of the present, expansionist period in Mormon history, the dead-end vision [of the lost generation] seems rather quaint."[21] But he adds a warning—that each generation has its own provinciality, that just as the views of those writers of the 1940s now seem as naive to us as their parents' views seemed to them, so our own views may appear naive to our children. It is certain that despite my criticism of various kinds of provincialism, I have my own kind. My best hope is to help us all guard against provinciality by suggesting additional possibilities, more and better perceived options, for our thinking about Mormonism and its literary tradition.

One other option, less provincial, I believe, because it is more inclusive than that of the Mormon novelists of the 1940s, is the direction taken by the third literary generation of rebels in my historical scheme. It is the second one within the past fifty years of renewed life in Mormon literature after the empty—or perhaps, given the harvest that followed, what could be called the "fallow"—middle fifty-year period. This generation overlaps with the "lost generation" somewhat and is, I believe, the one coming into flower right now, carrying my hope for the "dawning of a brighter day." These writers are characterized by various kinds and degrees of sincere commitment to the unique and demanding religious claims of Mormonism as well as to its people, history, and culture. Yet they are as clear-sighted and devastating in their analysis and criticism of Mormon mistakes and tragedies, both historical and present, as were the lost generation—in some cases *more* incisive because less naive and more empathetically involved themselves in Mormon conflicts and mistakes. For instance, Richard Bushman, in his important 1969 essay called "Faithful History," suggested some innovative, characteristically Mormon, approaches to writing history—one approach seeing the fundamental dramatic tension in religious history not (in the way most Mormon history has been written) as that between an all-righteous Church and an evil world but (as in fact most scriptural history is written) as that between God and his church. As Bushman describes it, "The Lord tries to establish his kingdom, but the stubborn people whom He favors with revelation ignore him much of the time and must be brought up short."[22] Here is one area where Mormon literature is perhaps ahead of Mormon historiography, because many of this latest generation of what I have called "rebels" are writing with just that perspective, focusing, like the prophets, on the struggles with faith and righteousness among the so-called chosen people as well as in the world. But, with these (unlike the "lost" generation), there is no patronization, no superior pointing of fingers, but rather full identification. They draw much of their power of specification from their own experience, their own conflicts and failures—and also from the redemptive charity that comes from their own genuine attempts in their own lives to repent, to live out the conflicts and sacrificial duties faith demands. Bushman concludes his essay with a suggestion that the finest Mormon history would be written not by writers who simply transfer various Mormon ideas or perspectives into their work, or who merely use certain techniques they think are Mormon, but by real changes in *all* things that shape their vision of the world in response to the self within which they encounter in moments of genuine faith. In a challenging inversion of the traditional Mormon axiom about being saved no faster than we gain knowledge, Bushman suggests that a Mormon cannot improve as a historian (I would add writer) without improving as a human being—in moral insight, spiritual commitment, and critical intelligence. As writers, "we gain knowledge no faster than we are saved." I believe this

In that sermon Joseph Smith also establishes—both through the theology and his literary creation—what seems the most promising central theme for Mormon literature: the search for self. I do not mean the unconscious revelation of various selves of the author, or the creation of personae, or the investigation of identity crises, all popular themes in recent literature, but rather the author's own successful search for and creation of his best personal resources in the process of his own writing. Mormon theology, as I have already suggested, provides the most radically individualistic doctrine of self accepted by any religion or philosophical persuasion. The Mormon ontology of self, contained in the doctrine of eternalism, is uniquely powerful to energize and direct aright the quest for self. That is why I believe Mormon theology is, all other things being equal, an aid toward better literature—and why Mormon literature would tend to be characterized by that quest.

Let me share an example of the search for self in our first generation of rebels, where the personal success and the literary success are interwoven. Eliza R. Snow's "Trail Diary," recording the exodus from Nauvoo to the Great Salt Lake, is known but not well enough known and is now out of print. She found her essential self in the black death and black mud of Winter Quarters, and in keeping her journal, as honestly and revealingly as she did, she provided one of the central values of good literature, a catalytic aid in our own search for self. The desperate trek across Iowa and then the Great Plains winter endured in caves and lean-to cabins was perhaps the most harrowing trial of the early Church. For those who did not die, or leave, it was a dark night of the soul and a being pushed back to basics, to frontiers of selfhood, from which they emerged discovered selves reborn. I feel certain this happened to Brigham Young. We have more direct evidence that it did to Eliza. What is most moving and to me makes her diary fine Mormon literature is not so much how much of self she

latest generation's growing quality is related to that kind of wholeness; they are finding out, tentatively and awkwardly, but surely, what it can mean for artistry to be a Latter-day Saint—a genuine follower of Christ.

But I wanted to get more specific about the literature itself. In the appendix following this essay, there is a checklist of what I judge to be the best Mormon literature, organized according to my scheme for a literary history and reflecting, of course, my own tastes and my interest in the theme of the search for self. Not only am I suggesting this as a valuable personal reading list for Mormons who are, for whatever natural reasons, interested in Mormon culture, but I suggest that almost all of these works are of sufficient quality that they could replace certain works of the same genre or period in anthologies or reading lists we use in our literature classes. While retaining the same or better literary quality they would provide an important *gain* in cultural and religious relevance for Mormon students. I will briefly comment on some outstanding and characteristic examples from each generation, mainly to whet your appetite.

It ought to mean something for Mormon literature that Mormonism *begins* with a book. But it is, of course, a book that has been laughed at, villified, and ignored—as well as one that has dramatically changed the lives of millions of people. Most surprising, despite its obvious verbal weight and complexity the Book of Mormon has until fairly recently not been carefully read as a *literary* text, even by Mormons. Ironically it was a *non-Mormon*, Douglas Wilson, who ten years ago reviewed this rather amazing situation and predicted that critical scrutiny from an "archetypal" perspective would be very productive.[23] That work has now begun and is proceeding apace: Bruce Jorgensen, Dill Rust, and George Tate have done some exciting work on the controlling mythic structures, the power and unity of the typological patterns (to use a concept from the book's narrators themselves) and their

controlling vision, centering on Lehi's dream as an archetypal source for much of the history and teaching of the
entire book. Others, such as Robert Thomas, Jack Welch,
and Steven Sondrup, have looked at specific poetic structures and at the rhetorical consistency and power which
even we who are the book's defenders, trained in quite a
different rhetorical tradition than that of the Hebrews, or
the nineteenth century, have tended to be somewhat
uneasy about. Steven Walker is even about to convince us
in print that its rhetorical concentration compares favor-
ably with the King James Bible, even when we include all
those "And it came to passes" and "Look and beholds." And
not only that, but a non-Mormon again, this time John
Seelye, the fine Melville scholar, has joined with Dil Rust
in a project to prepare and publish with a national press a
"Handbook of the Book of Mormon as Literature."

But what of the other early writings, those unquestionably by Joseph Smith himself? However we understand
the process of revelation, there are, of course, fine *passages*,
as literature, in the Doctrine and Covenants and the books
of Moses and Abraham. There are, for example, the impressive set pieces, like Sections 88 and 121 and the story
of Enoch. But what we still have not done is to take Joseph
Smith seriously as a *writer*, to be more like the Jews in
seeing scripture as the word of prophets as well as the
word of God, to let esthetic and rhetorical perceptions be
included in our response. Arthur Henry King claims to
have been originally moved far along toward his conversion
to the gospel by reading Joseph's own account of his
visions. As a trained and long-experienced stylistician, he
was convinced by Joseph's *style*—plain, cool, matter-of-fact,
unself-conscious—that he was telling the truth. Many less
sophisticated readers have *felt* the same thing, but we have
only scratched the surface in examining what this may
mean about the quality of literature available to us in
Joseph Smith's other writings—his letters and few
recorded sermons for instance—and in the writings of

other, equally uneducated but brilliantly perceptive and
transparent writers, from Brigham Young to Mary Goble
Pay.

Let me spend a moment on "The King Follett Discourse," perhaps the best piece of discursive literature yet
produced in the Church and one of the finest anywhere.
Fortunately, historians have stepped over into the neglected
stewardship of literary scholars to give us a professionally
amalgamated and edited text and have very helpfully
provided the historical and philosophical background that
enables us better to understand the sense of personal
vulnerability and of cosmic import that thrills us in the
sermon itself. But there still remains the task of literary
analysis and judgment that would promote wider reading
of this valuable text and better understanding of its
powerful literary qualities: the loosened and spontaneous,
characteristically Mormon, version of Puritan sermon
structure, the laying of a foundation stone for a Mormon
esthetic in references to the glory that dwells in matter,
the creation of enduring Mormon symbols, both visual and
sensual, such as Joseph's dramatically removing and using
his own ring as an image of eternal personal identity, his
talk of the *taste* of good doctrine and of the paradoxical
burnings (in the breast of the righteous *and* in the mind of
the damned). And finally this:

You never knew my heart. No man knows my history. I
cannot do it. I shall never undertake it . . . . If I had not
experienced what I have, I could not have believed it myself. I
never did harm any man since I have been born in the world.
My voice is always for peace. I cannot lie down until my work
is finished. I never think evil nor think anything to the harm
of my fellowman. When I am called at the trump and weighed
in the balance, you will know me then.[24]

We have here a piercing cry from a person discovering
himself, whom we do not yet know as fully as we might if
we knew him as a great writer.

exposes but what she reveals of the *process* of her unique discovery of self. We meet her at first as the spirited, intelligent and perceptive but also petulant, self-indulgent, and self-righteous young woman who had been Joseph Smith's secret wife and is now uncertain of her status. Nominally under Brigham Young's care, but shunted off to travel with a troubled family she guiltily detests, she is constantly seeking reassurance through blessings and counsel from such as Brigham Young and Heber C. Kimball.

But after the chastening of that winter a fine, patient strength, directness, and sense of humor slowly emerge, climaxing in the spring in one of the most remarkable outpourings of spiritual power and intelligence in religious history, among Eliza and others of the women of Winter Quarters. They taught each other by the spirit the doctrine of the kingdom and spoke and sang in tongues and laid their hands on the sick and afflicted sisters and blessed them to health. In September her wagon train met Brigham Young's group that was returning from the Salt Lake Valley settlement to Winter Quarters, where he would remain until spring, while she went on to Salt Lake. Of that meeting she writes:

Before the Pioneers left, Brigham came to the carriage and blest us. I ask'd who was to be my counsellor for the year to come. He said Eliza R. Snow. I said, "She is not capable." He said, "I have appointed her president."[25]

I see this passage as ironic and deeply revealing. Both she and Brigham Young knew that she had developed into a woman of incredible spiritual daring and stature and had a resulting self-confidence and sense of self that could allow her to playfully pretend to her former dependence—but with complete assurance, in both of them, that she was, whether he appointed her or not, indeed president of her own soul.

We have yet to explore in our literature, our fiction

and poetry and drama, the most demanding spiritual frontiers for *modern* Mormons, possible equivalents to those Brigham Young found—and created—on the physical frontiers of our beginnings as a people that produced the authentic personal literature of that time. One place that *can* stimulate an authentic search for self, one that can be true to our theology as well as our deepest reality and needs, is the mission field. I mean of course not that pale, demeaning search most often meant in our time when someone says that self-indulgent "I want to get in touch with my real self," and then, too often with expensive self-help therapy, defines himself by his worst imaginings, doubts, and desires, as if his truest self were a static minimum, his lowest common denominator, which he must then conform to. I mean rather that discovery of one's inner dynamic, his creatable and creative core, his eternally grounded potential, his swelling, growing seed-self.

With such a focus, the missionary experience, as reality and archetype, can do more for Mormon life and letters than serve as an exotic area for exploring religious identity crises. Of course, it is natural and necessary that modern Mormon writers find their true subject matter and their craft in their own way. But there *are* useful models: what I am suggesting has already been done remarkably well in some missionary diaries, such as that of Joseph Millett. He gives us a day-by-day account of his discovery and development of self as an eighteen-year-old called on a mission in 1852, who made his way alone and mainly afoot across the continent to Nova Scotia, found his Savior on his own, learned the gospel, developed his own resources, and lived a life of remarkable spiritual perception and of pure service. An entry at the end of his journal, chosen from an earlier experience to summarize his life, captures the central moral vision and sense of self acquired by one who has lived a true religion. His life is capped both religiously and artistically by his creation of this anecdote from the hard days of his settlement of Spring Valley, Nevada, where he was called to pioneer by Brigham Young after he returned from his mission and where his daughter had died and many had suffered great sickness and hunger:

> . . . one of my children came in, said that Brother Newton Hall's folks were out of bread. Had none that day. I put . . . our flour in sack to send up to Brother Hall's. Just then Brother Hall came in. Says I, "Brother Hall, how are you out for flour." "Brother Millett, we have none." "Well, Brother Hall, there is some in that sack. I have divided and was going to send it to you. Your children told mine that you were out." Brother Hall began to cry. Said he had tried others. Could not get any. Went to the cedars and prayed to the Lord and the Lord told him to go to Joseph Millett. "Well, Brother Hall, you needn't bring this back if the Lord sent you for it. You don't owe me for it." You can't tell how good it made me feel to know that the Lord knew that there was such a person as Joseph Millett.[26]

That anecdote not only created a new version of what it means to find oneself through losing oneself, but embodied it movingly in real experience, authentically and artistically recreated in words—certainly fine literature.

The "lost generation's" literary achievement was almost totally in fiction, and the finest examples are Maureen Whipple's *The Giant Joshua* and Virginia Sorensen's *The Evening and the Morning*. *Joshua* is one of the richest, fullest, most moving, *truest* fictions about the pioneer experience of anyone, not just Mormons. But Whipple finally remains too much a part of that second major generation of Mormon writers, like them properly energized by her independence and disillusionment with her people and Church but not finally reconciled to her characters and subject in the way great art requires. The novel falls off badly in the last hundred pages—her powerful theme of human struggle and her fine central characters are a victim of the sentimental Emersonian Romanticism she substitutes for a genuine Mormon theology, and finally the muscular plot is betrayed by melodrama. But if it is true, as some say, that one cannot understand the Mormon experience without understanding the struggle of the Dixie Mission—the human cost and the faith that was willing to meet the cost and the human results won in the struggle, then we have in *The Giant Joshua* a most direct and perceptive means for understanding Mormon experience. It is our finest fictional access to our roots as Mormons and as Rocky Mountain, high-desert people, our most profound imaginative knowledge of the spiritual ancestors of all Mormons, the Dixie pioneers.

Virginia Sorensen's novel, if not quite as remarkable as Whipple's flawed masterpiece, is certainly the best novel yet about twentieth-century Mormon experience. Sorensen shares some of Whipple's "lost generation" flaws, a certain patronizing attitude toward Mormon thought, which she obviously does not understand too well. It occurs to me, for instance, that Sorensen, and her protagonist Kate Alexander, understand sin very well, its complex beginnings in small, tragic misunderstandings and impulses, its way of continuing even when the pains and costs become much greater than the pleasures and rewards. But Sorensen does not understand the Atonement—the processes, costs, and unique Christian resources that make up repentance. On the other hand, our first generation seems to have understood the Atonement quite well, at least its power in their initial change as they came out of the world into Zion. But they apparently did not understand much about individual sin—the "mystery of iniquity"—and its continuing challenge in their lives. My greater hope for the third generation of writers is because they understand sin well enough—both that of the world and their own—and they also understand the Atonement and can struggle to make its grandeur part of their art. Sorensen once identified herself with writers "in the middle—incapable of severe orthodoxies."[27] I think the greatest Mormon literature will be written by those who, like the first generation, are capable of severe orthodoxies, but who are also able to transcend the narrowness and limitations this implies into new freedom, enlarged possibilities. Some are learning this, and one fine place for them—and their potential audience—to learn is from *The Evening and the Morning*. As Ed Geary has commented, we are not likely to have better novels than those of the 1940s until we learn what they have to teach.[28] One besides Geary who is helping us is Bruce Jorgensen, who has written—about *The Evening and the Morning*, why it is Mormon and what it achieves—one of the subtlest and most useful pieces of literary criticism I have read.[29]

Eileen Kump is one in the *third* generation who has shown her ability to learn from her Mormon literary tradition and go beyond; her few slowly crafted stories, especially "The Willows" (on a smaller scale than *Giant Joshua* but without its problems), reach the heights of Whipple's achievements with fiction as a mode of historical apprehension.[30] Thayer and Marshall have shown what they have learned in remarkable meditations on initiation into the complexities of inner evil and on the demands of outer reality, including one's family and community. And younger writers of fiction are coming along with authentic skills and also the grounding in Mormon thought and conviction that I think characterizes the third generation. I will mention only one example, the finely tuned, uncompromising but compassionate story about a young Mormon mother recently published by Dian Saderup.[31] These writers still have some things to learn from the second generation, mainly about handling significant Mormon materials on a large canvas, the size of a novel.

That process of learning from but moving beyond the second generation has in some ways been more fully accomplished by our poets, but they still face some of the same great challenges and could also use much more of our support and help. Clinton Larson was the first real Mormon poet, the groundbreaker for the third literary generation in achieving a uniquely Mormon poetic, and is still, by virtue of both quantity and quality of work, our foremost literary artist. He is a writer I respect and love for both his genius and his personal sacrifice in making his difficult and costly way essentially alone. Certainly only a part of his work is first-rate (about the same proportion as in Dickinson or Whitman). But he has produced a significant number and variety of poems that will stand with the best written by anyone in his time: for instance "Homestead in Idaho," which captures with great power unique qualities of our pioneer heritage—that intense, faith-testing loneliness and loss, that incredible will to take chances and their consequences, even to be defeated, the challenge posed by experience to our too easy security within the plan, the seeing how the tragic implications of our theology are borne out in mortality. And Larsen's range goes all the way from that long narrative work to a perfectly cut jewel like "To a Dying Girl."[32] That poem, which is included at the back of this essay, develops, with the ultimately irrational, unanalyzable poignancy of pure lyricism, the same theme that preoccupied Emily Dickinson in her finest work—the incomprehensible, imperceptible change of being from one state to another, symbolized most powerfully for her in the change of seasons, but felt most directly in the mysterious, adamant change of death. Her best work on this theme, such as "Farther in Summer than the Birds" and "There's a Certain Slant of Light," lives in the mind as a constant antidote to both sentimentality and despair about death's change. Larson uses a wider multiplicity of images ("She moves like evening into night,/ Forgetful as the swans forget their flight"), but with similiar metrical brilliance, varying the line lengths to bring up the rhymes in special intervals and dropping the first slack syllable from certain of his pentameter lines in order to image the balanced hesitation and release of emotion he wants to create. Read it a few times and it will live in your mind as surely and deservedly as Dickinson's best work.

Another poem I have printed following this essay, "Advent," shows Larson with the characteristic voice of the third generation, evoking the elegant, hypocritically materialistic modern Christians, including Mormons, who expect to welcome a gentle Christ, domesticated to their values—but who will be as surprised as everyone else at the overwhelming reality. Also at the end of the essay are poems by two younger poets showing characteristic third-generation handling of historical and devotional Mormon themes and variety of stylistic techniques.

The differences I have described between the first and third generations are well exemplified in the differences between the essays produced by the two groups. The first generation was too uniformly embattled against the outside world for the kinds of complex revelations of personal feelings and differences, or the subtle examinations of more universal problems existing *within* as well as without the Church, that characterize the modern Mormon personal essay. Only a beginning has been made at characterizing this genre and evaluating its examples, but we have Mary Bradford's provocative analyses of what has been written[33] and Ed Geary's and Laurel Ulrich's and others' experiments with the form. The experiments show how the essay can work not so much to convey information as give the reader vicarious experience (like other forms of imaginative literature) and yet still retain its unique abilities to deal directly with the most challenging dimensions of Mormon theology.

For instance, as Clifton Jolley has pointed out, Mormon thought exposes those who know it and take it seriously to the consequences of living in an ultimately paradoxical universe, where opposition must needs be or otherwise there is no existence, where God cannot achieve his purposes through will alone and therefore has problems and suffers, not only through choice but through necessity, where he has power to bring salvation with our cooperation but not without it. The consequences include terror and awful responsibility as well as the hope of exciting eternal adventure. The Mormon personal essay can have both a substantive and a formal advantage over any other approach to the terror of life because, while lacking somewhat the *indirection* in other forms, it can combine many of their other virtues (the rich textural element of fiction, for instance) without separating itself from the directness and responsibility involved in dealing with the *literally* true, as well as *fictively* true, experience. As Jolley writes, "The personal essay is utterly responsible, its point of view is owned. In it, one may take neither comfort nor refuge in the satisfaction of pose or form; one must face the beast, naked and alone."[34] I have faith that the personal essay, developed into new dimensions and powers by Mormon writers, may serve as our most productive genre, the one best tuned to the particular strengths and tendencies of Mormon thought and experience, including of course the search for self. It provides naturally for the widest possible appreciation by Mormon readers and the widest involvement by Mormon writers because of its accessible but powerful form, and it may well be our most important contribution to the wider world literary culture.

Now let me conclude with some problems and possibilities. Our major need, in order to keep up with and perhaps encourage the dawning of a brighter day, is for teachers of literature to engage in serious study, critical and scholarly writing about, and the use in their teaching of the best of our developing literary heritage. This will help make encouragement and resources available to our writers and will help develop the understanding and appreciative audience they need. And I don't suggest carping at the didactic or sentimental Mormon literature we don't like, coming from the Church presses and Church magazines. If we do our job in providing successively better understanding of alternatives, all that reading of what we think of as inferior stuff won't hurt anyone. To paraphrase Brother Brigham, "I would rather that persons read [sentimental] novels—than read nothing."[35] But we also have a large, more subtle, and potentially more widely valuable task: I realize that the challenge of properly relating scholarship and artistic achievement to moral character or religious faith—of connecting truth and goodness to beauty—is a huge and treacherous one, one that has not been resolved with very great success by many, historically or in the world at large at present. But I find at BYU a surprising lack of interest in trying to resolve it, an almost secularist distrust, particularly in the social sciences and humanities, of any attempt to directly apply gospel perspectives and standards to scholarship or artistry. Part of that distrust stems from a very proper revulsion at seeing such combinations made naively or superficially or self-righteously (as some may have done at BYU), but we at this university are untrue to our professional responsibilities as well as our faith if we do not somehow come to terms with the charge given us by the Chairman of our Board of Trustees, President Spencer W. Kimball, in his "Second Century Address" at BYU:

We surely cannot give up our concerns with character and conduct without also giving up on mankind. Much misery results from flaws in character, not from failures in technology. We cannot give in to the ways of the world with regard to the realm of art. . . . Our art must be the kind which edifies man, which takes into account his immortal nature, and which prepares us for heaven, not hell.[36]

I feel certain President Kimball was not talking about simple piety, superficial Mormonism of the kind our home literature has fostered. Later that day when he asked the Lord to "let the morality of the graduates of this University provide the music of hope for the inhabitants of this planet,"[37] it was a beautiful and lucid but also very challenging moment that we have not yet come to terms with. And we *will* not if we on the one hand resist that charge as too pious and unacademic for serious scholars or on the other hand think it only has to do with the Word of Wisdom and dress standards, rather than the serious and extremely difficult moral issues our graduates will face in the world—such as the increasingly shrill and violent struggles of various groups for and against certain "rights," the overwhelming hopelessness of the poor and ignorant and suppressed, and "the wars and the perplexities of the nations" (Doctrine and Covenants 88:79).

President Kimball was speaking in a great tradition of the latter-day prophets, a tradition that we sometimes forget. Listen to Brigham Young:

There is not, has not been, and never can be any method, scheme, or plan devised by any being in this world for intelligence to eternally exist and obtain an exaltation, without knowing the good and the evil—without tasting the bitter and the sweet. Can the people understand that it is actually necessary for opposite principles to be placed before them, or this state of being would be no probation, and we should have no opportunity for exercising the agency given us? Can they understand that we cannot obtain eternal life unless we actually know and comprehend by our experience the principle of good and the principle of evil, the light and the darkness, truth, virtue, and holiness—also vice, wickedness and corruption?[38]

Or listen to Joseph Smith:

The things of God are of deep import; and time, and experience, and careful and ponderous and solemn thoughts can only find them out. Thy mind, O Man! if thou wilt lead a soul unto salvation, must stretch as high as the utmost heavens, and search into and contemplate the darkest abyss and the broad expanse of eternity.[39]

Nothing superficial or pious or sentimental there; it would be hard to find better statements of what the greatest, the most *challenging*, literature and other works of art succeed in doing. But in fact we tend officially at BYU to resist this

doctrinal tradition—the need to actually know and comprehend by our experience the principle of good and the
principle of evil, to search into and contemplate the darkest
abyss and the broad expanse of eternity; instead we engage
in practices and policies that seem aimed more at preserving
innocence than developing virtue, at protection rather
than progression. These practices and policies may at this
time be necessary, given other important values of the
Church—such as protecting the blamelessly naive, like
new converts, and maintaining a certain image before the
world and before BYU's general LDS constituency, including parents and alumni. Therefore, we may have to
wait until we are mature enough to have a genuine Zion
culture before we can deal *directly* with these challenges.
But some resolution to this dilemma lies in more effective
use of the arts, especially literature, drama, and film,
where virtue and vice can be represented not as direct, raw
experience, with all its power to overwhelm, even destroy,
the fragile soul, but as experience mediated through the
moral understanding, as well as the technical mastery, of
the artist.

And for these purposes the kind of art I have been
describing and proposing to you—that is, genuine Mormon
literature—is, I believe, one of our richest and most direct
resources. Literature has unique and long-proven ability
to teach not only moral rigor and sensitivity but to teach
specific moral intelligence. For instance, I think the more
particular relevance of *The Evening and the Morning* to
Mormon thought and experience, compared say to *Anna
Karenina*, can compensate for its somewhat inferior artistic
qualities, compared to that great novel, and make it
therefore a similarly rich and valuable resource for bringing
us to actually know and comprehend by our imaginative
experience the principle of good and principle of evil
involved in judging adultery and still caring about an
adulteress.

And I think we can and will produce even better

literature, on this and other themes. Wallace Stegner, in his famous essay on Western writers, "Born a Square," laments of such writers, including himself (and I think it is essentially true of Mormondom's lost generation), "We cannot find, apparently, a present and living society that is truly ours and that contains the materials of a deep commitment."[40] I suspect that "the great Mormon novel" some still yearn for will be written by someone in what I have called the "third generation" who is at peace with the Mormon past and at home in its present yet who has developed both the critical objectivity and the artistic flexibility to mold the raw materials of the Mormon tradition and Mormon thought into the paradoxical texture of good fiction. She, or he, will have a balance of both individual and community integrity, will have 20-20 vision in both the eye of faith and the eye of knowledge, will see the faults without rancor or self-righteous pride and the virtues without sentimentality or self-consciousness. The writers of the great—the good—Mormon novels (or plays or biographies or books of poems) will be those whose human conscience remains sensitive and courageous but whose wounds have healed.

Doug Thayer commented to me recently, as we discussed the problems still to be solved in the efforts he and others are making to do what the Mormon novel theoretically could do, "When we can solve them, when we find out how to handle our real subject matter, things will just burst open in Mormon fiction." I think he is right. But we who are the teachers, the critics, the literate audience— what can we do to help, and what can we avoid that will hinder? We must *not* do some of the things I may seem guilty of in this essay—be overly optimistic, too easy in our criticism, slothful in our expectations of what a truly Mormon literature will be and will cost. I trust I am not guilty. I have been trying to show that it is *not easier* to be a good Christian or Mormon writer, but more difficult; piety will not take the place of inner gifts or tough thinking or hard training and work.

The dangers of mixing religion and art are clear and present—from both sides. Literature is not a substitute for religion and making it such is a sure road to hell; and just as surely religious authority is no substitute for honest literary perception and judgment, and didactic, apologetic, or sentimental writing, however "true" in some literal sense, is no substitute for real literature in its power to grasp and change. In the direction of such sentimentalism lies spiritual suicide. We must stop rewarding the "pious trash," as Flannery O'Connor called much Catholic literature—a phrase that well describes much of our own; and we must, on the other hand, also stop awarding prizes to those stories which, for instance, in reaching for unearned maturity, use sexual explicitness or sophomoric skepticism as faddish, but phony, symbols of intellectual and moral sophistication and freedom—or merely to titillate their prudish Mormon audience. Various forms of Scylla and Charybdis threaten all about, and we must proceed with some caution along straight and narrow courses.

But we should also have the courage of our supposed convictions: People outside the Church are calling Mormonism such things as "the only successful American religious movement" or recognizing Joseph Smith as the most interesting religious mind in America or Brigham Young as one of the world's most impressive empire builders and practical thinkers. Many of us have even stronger convictions about the inherent greatness and interest of our heritage and its people. We now need to be at least as willing as some of our non-Mormon friends to follow out the professional consequences: to do the scholarship, the recovery and explication of texts, the writing of biographies, the literary criticism and theorizing, the teaching—even the simple reading—that will help bring to full flower a culture commensurate with our great religious and historical roots.

Advent

The gentle God is our guest;
His staff will prompt us to the door.
The table is set in the oak-paneled room:
Goblets are rinsed and set out,
The warm vapor vanishing around them;
The silver, withdrawn from felt-lined mahogany,
Is counted and burnished to mercurial white
And set on immaculate linen,
Sleek with crystal and rococo ware.

The table is set for the Guest
Near the imminent door.
The servants stalk
Each gray indiscretion to be rent
On the merciless rack of their decor.

The table is set for the gentle God:
The roasted fowl entice the savoring tongue;
The marmalade and sweetmeats brim
The centerpiece, a horn;
The fruit is full, plucked in prime,
Oranges, apples, pears
Like noon-shade autumn leaves.
The supper will please the gentle God
Who surely comes,
Who comes like the breath on a veil.

But out of the East the breath is fire!
Who comes with temblor, sound of hurricane?
Who rages on the portico?
Who claps his vengeful steel on stone?
Who comes to dine?

The servants cower like quail in the anterooms.
Who blasphemes in the shuddering halls?
Who rends the imminent door?
Our guest is a gentle God, a Lamb.

—Clinton F. Larson

Reprinted from *The Lord of Experience*, (Brigham Young University Press, 1967) by special permission of the author.

To a Dying Girl

How quickly must she go?
She calls dark swans from mirrors everywhere:
From halls and porticos, from pools of air.
How quickly must she know?
They wander through the fathoms of her eye,
Waning southerly until their cry
Is gone where she must go.
How quickly does the cloudfire streak the sky,
Tremble on the peaks, then cool and die?
She moves like evening into night,
Forgetful as the swans forget their flight
Or spring the fragile snow,
So quickly she must go.

—Clinton F. Larson

Reprinted from *The Lord of Experience*, (Brigham Young University Press, 1967) by special permission from the author.

A Litany for the Dark Solstice

Dead of winter,
Dead of night,
Neither center,
Left, nor right.

Teach me error
Within reason;
Stay me with terror
Out of season.
When I have most,
Whirl it as dust.
Salt be the taste
Of all I love best
in earth, and rust
Be the iron I trust.

In my distress,
Bless me to bless.
On urgent water,
Gone oar and rudder,
Still me this rest:

Break me to Christ.

—Bruce F. Jorgensen

Letter to a Four-Year-Old Daughter

The days you instill in me only exhaustion,
reverberating from living room walls,
leaping, hanging, hurling as you instruct,
"Listen but don't look—tell me what this hits!"
I force my eyes to look calmly at a coloring book,
stained-glass with fifty colors patched on a waxy duck,

and send you off to sing, riding breakneck
on your toy horse to rhythms of "I am a child
of God", leaving me penitent in my fatigue.
As you compose, "Joseph Smith was a good prophet . . ."
I recall with renewal the day at your insistence
you learned how he was murdered. Refusing evasion,

you required whole truth, scorning attempts
at explanation, tolerance, and a happy ending
in heaven; you choked down scrambled eggs, weeping,
"But they didn't have to kill him," and again
at bedtime, "they didn't have to kill him."
Like Porter Rockwell, one of few, you inquired,

"Who were they, what were their names?"
Now, horse providing percussion, you end your song,
"It was so long ago, we don't know their names,
don't know their names." In a sudden double-exposure
I glimpse a hounded man—a prophet—and a blond head
bowed for blood that shines from a newly found grave.

—Linda Sillitoe

Reprinted by permission from BYU Studies 16 (Winter, 1976): 234.

Notes

1. Richard Cracroft and Neal Lambert, *A Believing People: Literature of the Latter-day Saints* (Provo, Utah: Brigham Young University Press, 1974; reprint, Salt Lake City: Bookcraft, 1979).

2. See appended bibliography.

3. Paul Cracroft, *A Certain Testimony* (Salt Lake City: Epic West, 1979).

4. Bruce Jorgensen, "Born of the Water," *Sunstone*, 5 (January-February 1980): 20-25.

5. Bela Petsco, *Nothing Very Important and Other Stories* (Provo, Utah: Meservydale Publishing Co., 1979).

6. Edward Geary, "Goodbye to Poplarhaven," *Dialogue: A Journal of Mormon Thought* 8 (Summer 1973): 56-62; reprinted in Cracroft and Lambert, *A Believing People*, pp. 242-47.

7. Edward Geary, "Hying to Kolob," *Dialogue* 13 (Fall 1980): 93-101.

8. Flannery O'Connor, "The Church and the Fiction Writer," in *Mystery and Manners*, eds. Sally and Robert Fitzgerald (New York: Farrar, Straus, and Giroux, 1969), p. 148, quoted in Karl Keller, "The Example of Flannery O'Connor,"*Dialogue* 9 (Winter 1974): 62.

9. Keller, p. 62.

10. Ibid., p. 68

11. Stan Larson, "The King Follett Discourse: A New Amalgamated Text," *Brigham Young University Studies* 18 (Winter 1978): 204.

12. W. S. Merwin, "Come Back," quoted and discussed in Robert Pinsky, *The Situation of Poets* (Princeton: Princeton University Press, 1976), p. 95.

13. B. F. Cummings, *The Eternal Individual Self* (Salt Lake City: Utah Publishing Co., 1968), pp. 7, 69, 70, quoted in Bruce Jorgensen, "'Herself Moving Beside Herself, Out There Alone': The Shape of Mormon Belief in Virginia Sorensen's *The Evening and the Morning*," *Dialogue* 13 (Fall 1980): 43-61.

14. Stephen Tanner, "Literature and Creeds," (unpublished essay).

15. Parley P. Pratt, "The Morning Breaks," in *Hymns* (Salt Lake City: Deseret Press, 1948), p. 269.

16. Cracroft and Lambert, *A Believing People*, pp. 143-50.

17. Orson F. Whitney, "Home Literature," *Contributor* (July 1888) reprinted in Cracroft and Lambert, *A Believing People*, pp. 204-05.

18. Edward Geary, "The Poetics of Provincialism: Mormon Regional Fiction," *Dialogue* 18 (Summer 1978): 15.

19. Edward Geary, "Mormondom's Lost Generation: The Novelists of the 1940s," *Brigham Young University Studies* 18 (Fall 1977): 89-98.

20. Dale L. Morgan, "Literature in the History of the Church: The Importance of Involvement," *Dialogue* 4 (Autumn 1969): 31.

21. Geary, "The Poetics of Provincialism," p. 24.

22. Richard L. Bushman, "Faithful History," *Dialogue* 4 (Winter 1969): 18.

23. Douglas Wilson, "Prospects for the Study of the Book of Mormon as a Work of American Literature," *Dialogue* 4 (Winter 1969): 18.

24. Stan Larson, "The King Follett Discourse: A Newly Amalgamated Text," ibid., p. 208.

25. Eliza R. Snow, *Eliza R. Snow an Immortal: Selected Writings* (Salt Lake City: Nicholas G. Morgan Foundation, 1957), p. 346.

26. "The Journal of Joseph Millett," LDS Church Archives, partially reprinted in Eugene England, "A Nineteen-Year-Old Missionary in Nova Scotia," *New Era* (June 1975), p. 28, and Eugene England, "Great Books or True Religion? Defining the Mormon Scholar," *Dialogue* 9 (Winter 1974): 46.

27. Virginia Sorensen, "Is It True—The Novelist and His Materials," *Western Humanities Review* 7 (1953): 290-91.

28. Geary, "The Poetics of Provincialism," p. 24.

29. Jorgensen, "'Herself Moving Beside Herself, Out There Alone,'" op. cit.

30. Eileen Kump, *Bread and Milk* (Provo, Utah: Brigham Young University Press, 1979).

31. Dian Saderup, "A Blessing of Duty," *Sunstone*, 4 (May 1979): 17-20.

32. Clinton F. Larson, *The Lord of Experience* (Provo, Utah: Brigham Young University Press, 1967), p. 21.

33. Mary Bradford, "I, Eye, Aye: A Personal Essay on Personal Essays," *Dialogue* 11 (Summer 1978): 81-89.

34. Clifton Holt Jolley, "Mormons and the Beast," *Dialogue* 11 (Autumn 1978): 138.

35. A slight change from how he is quoted in Hugh Nibley, "Educating the Saints—A Brigham Young Mosaic," in Cracroft and Lambert, *A Believing People*, p. 226.

36. Spencer W. Kimball, "Second Century Address," *Brigham Young University Studies* 16 (Summer 1976): 457.

37. Ibid.

38. Brigham Young et al., *Journal of Discourses*, 26 vols. (London, 1854-86), 7: 237.

39. Joseph Smith, "Letter to the Church from Liberty Jail, March 1839," *History of the Church*, ed. B. H. Roberts, 6 vols. (Salt Lake City: Deseret News Press, 1930), 3: 295.

40. Wallace Stegner, "Born a Square," *The Sound of Mountain Water* (Garden City, N. Y.: Doubleday, 1969), p. 178.

A Select Bibliography of Mormon Literature

[Critical reviews in brackets]

ANTHOLOGIES

Richard Cracroft and Neal Lambert, *A Believing People* (1974 and 1979) (hereafter cited *C & L*); *Twenty-two Young Mormon Writers* (1975); [Bruce Jorgensen, "Digging the Foundation," *Dialogue* (Winter 1974); Eugene England, Review, *BYU Studies* (Spring 1975)].

FIRST GENERATION(1830-1880)
The Book of Mormon
[Bruce Jorgensen, "The Dark Way to the Tree," *Encyclia*, vol. 54, part 2, 1977].

Diaries
George Laub, *BYU Studies* (Winter 1978); Joseph Millett, *The New Era* (June 1975); Eliza R. Snow, *Selected Writings* (1957) [Neal Lambert, "The Representation of Reality in Mormon Autobiography," *Dialogue* (Summer 1978)].

Autobiography
Joseph Smith, *Pearl of Great Price* and *History of the Church; The Autobiography of Parley P. Pratt* (1888); [R. A. Christmas, "The Autobiography of PPP," *Dialogue* (Spring 1966)].

Letters
Dear Ellen edited by George S. Ellsworth, (University of Utah, 1974); *My Dear Son: . . . Brigham Young to his Sons* (Desert Book, 1974) [William Mulder, Review, *Dialogue* (Winter 1974)]; *Twelve Mormon Homes*, Elizabeth Kane (University of Utah, 1974).

Sermons
Joseph Smith, "King Follett Discourse," Amalgamated Text and Scholarly Articles, *BYU Studies* (Winter 1978); *Journal of Discourses* (26 vols., 1854-86); *Discourses of Brigham Young* (1925).

MIDDLE ("FALLOW") PERIOD (1880-1930)

"Home Literature"
(Expressly for LDS, to increase faith; mainly in Church magazines.) Nephi Anderson, *Added Upon* (Deseret, 1898); stories by Anderson and Josephine Spencer in *C & L*; Eliza R. Snow, *Poems* (1877); Orson F. Whitney, *Elias, An Epic* (1904); and *Poetical Writings* (1889).

History
B. H. Roberts, *Comprehensive History of the Church* (6 vols., 1930).

Theology
B. H. Roberts, *Joseph Smith Prophet-Teacher* (1908) and *Seventies Course in Theology* (1907); John A. Widtsoe, *A Rational Theology* (1915).

SECOND ("LOST") GENERATION (1930-1960)

Fiction
Virginia Sorensen, *The Evening and the Morning* (1949) and *Where Nothing Is Long Ago* (stories, 1963), especially "The Darling Lady," *C & L*; Maureen Whipple, *The Giant Joshua* (1941 and 1977); Samuel Taylor, *Heaven Knows Why* (comic novel, 1948 and 1979); [Edward Geary, "The Poetics of Provincialism: Mormon Regional Fiction," *Dialogue* (Summer 1978); Bruce Jorgensen, "The Shape of Mormon Belief in Virginia Sorenson's *The Evening . . .*" *Dialogue* (Fall 1980); 43-61. Bruce Jorgensen, "Retrospection: *Giant Joshua*," *Sunstone* (1978); Richard Cracroft, "Freshet in the Dearth: S. Taylor's *Heaven Knows Why* and "Mormon Humor," *Proceedings of the Association for Mormon Letters*, 1978].

THIRD GENERATION (1960-)

Poetry
Clinton Larson, *The Lord of Experience* (1967), *The Mantle of the Prophet and Other Plays* (1966), and *The Western World* (1978); see especially poems at end of essay and "Letter from Israel Whiton,

1851," *C & L;* "Homestead in Idaho," (*Lord of Experience*), and from *The Western World* "Jesse" and "Lovers at Twilight"; [John B. Harris, Review, *BYU Studies* (Winter 1968); Karl Keller, "A Pilgrimage of Awe," *Dialogue* (Autumn 1968); Thomas Schwartz, "Sacrament of Terror: Violence in the Poetry of Clinton Larson," *Dialogue* (Autumn 1974)]; Emma Lou Thayne, *Spaces in the Sage* (1971); John S. Harris, *Barbed Wire* (1974); Edward Hart, *To Utah* (1979); Marden Clark, *Moods, Of Late* (1979); see also Carol Lynn Pearson, Bruce Jorgensen, Linda Sillitoe, Clifton Jolley, Elouise Bell, and Dennis Clark in various periodicals.

Fiction
Douglas Thayer, *Under the Cottonwoods* (1977), and "Red-tailed Hawk," *Dialogue* (Autumn 1969); Don Marshall, *The Rummage Sale* (1972) and *Frost in the Orchard* (1977); Eileen Kump, *Bread and Milk* (1980); Bela Petsco, *Nothing Important . . .* (1979); Dian Saderup, "A Blessing of Duty," *Sunstone* (May 1979).

Personal Essay
Nibley on the Timely and the Timeless (1979); Edward Geary, "Goodbye to Poplarhaven," *C & L;* "Personal Voices" section in many issues of *Dialogue* after 1971; Carole Hansen, "The Death of a Son" *Dialogue* (Autumn 1967); Karl Keller, "Every Soul Has Its South," *Dialogue* (Summer 1966); Levi Peterson, "The Mormons and Wilderness," *Sunstone* (December 1979); [Mary Bradford, "I, Eye, Aye . . ." *Dialogue* (Summer 1979); Clifton Jolley, "Mormons and the Beast," *Dialogue* (Autumn 1978)].

Drama
Robert Elliot, "Fires of the Mind," *Sunstone* (Winter 1975); Tom Rogers, "Huebner" and "Reunion"; [Review of contemporary Mormon drama by "Bliss and Gump," *Sunstone* (Spring 1976)].

General
Eugene England, "Great Books or True Religion?" *Dialogue* (Winter 1974); special issues on Mormon literature in *Dialogue* (Winter 1972, Winter 1974, and Summer 1977).

Biography
Edward and Andrew Kimball, *Spencer W. Kimball* (1977); [Review, Eugene England and Charles Tate, *BYU Studies* (Summer 1978)].

History
Arrington, Fox, and May, *Building the City of God* (1976); Arrington and Bitton, *The Mormon Experience* (1979). [Richard L. Bushman, "Faithful History," *Dialogue* (Winter, 1969).]

Folklore
Austin Fife, *Saints of Sage and Saddle* (1956); special issue on folklore of *Utah Historical Quarterly* (Fall 1976); on the nature of folklore: William A. (Bert) Wilson, "The Paradox of Mormon Folklore," *BYU Studies* (Autumn 1976).

5

The Church Moves Outside the United States: Some Observations from Latin America

F. LaMond Tullis

The recent extraordinary growth of the Church in areas of the world in which missionaries have traditionally had considerable difficulty has occasioned comment and speculation. New members are now flocking into the Church in Taiwan, Japan, Portugal, Italy, and Mexico, while traditional fields of harvest in England, Scandinavia, and Germany have turned fallow. In the following essay, F. LaMond Tullis, Professor of Political Science and Chairman of the Department of Political Science at Brigham Young University, comments on the unprecedented rate of growth in Latin America and then focuses on some of the troubling consequences of this rapid expansion.

Selecting the themes of nationalism and authority, Professor Tullis considers problems such as cultural conflict, imperialism, and indigenous leadership styles. Thus the boast that the American flag is God's flag has won few friends and many enemies when Latin American Saints view it against the cultural, economic, and military imperialism of the colossus of the north. Equally counterproductive has been the attempt to impose North American cultural stereotypes on the Latin Americans' ethos. Just as serious for the smooth operation of wards and branches has been the adaptation of Latin American leadership styles that emphasize personal authority and machismo to a religious organization based on personal testimony and voluntary membership.

That the Church of Jesus Christ of Latter-day Saints has been enormously successful in Latin America is true. That it faces difficulties in consolidating those successes and transferring membership statistics into stable wards and stakes is also true. This is a problem that early nineteenth-century Church leaders faced but that Latter-day Saints have not generally encountered in recent years. With the emphasis on the gathering that continued until the late 1950s, members came to Zion, were integrated into existing wards, and were acculturated to North American norms. Now, the Latter-day Saints face the challenge of creating multiple Zions in cultures far removed from the predominantly northern European culture of the United States. If the Church is to succeed in fulfilling the much-quoted prophecy of Daniel to roll forth and fill the earth, it must meet the challenge of multiple cultures as successfully as it met the challenge of acculturating non-American immigrants in times past.

Mormons of the present generation, with their legacy of tenacity and perseverance as both a guide and a challenge, are attempting to offer "every nation, kindred, tongue, and people" an opportunity to hear the gospel of Jesus Christ. The scale of this endeavor is new to us, for never before has the Church attempted to take the gospel message across as many boundaries of ancestral customs, languages, nationalities, and races as now. The magnitude of such an attempt—and the drama that it represents—has presented new problems. For one, the diversity of membership we are experiencing in the Church is both blessing and challenging the collective spirit of Mormonism. Change is upon us, and we must try to understand it and deal with it in both spirit and mind.

Certainly Latin America deserves our attention. There, more than 600,000 members reside in eighteen of the twenty-three independent Latin American republics and Puerto Rico. Currently the region is experiencing the highest rate of membership growth in the Church. In 1975 Mexico alone accounted for over 22 percent of the baptisms in the Church. That was with 21,000 converts. In 1976 Mexico had 40,000 converts. Other Latin American countries, though less dramatic, are not far behind. In Latin America indigenous roots have now taken hold—

some of them deeply—and Mormonism more and more is becoming recognized as a national asset.

In 1960 all Spanish- and Portuguese-speaking members of the Church combined in Latin America accounted for only 1½ percent of the Church's total membership. Yet by 1971 that total had risen to 7 percent, and by 1975 to over 9 percent. By early 1979 that percentage had risen to 12.17 percent. In 1990 one out of every five members of the Mormon faith may speak Spanish or Portugese as his or her mother tongue. Inasmuch as the Church's membership is growing rapidly among many language groups throughout much of the world, this progressive Latin American gain is quite remarkable, exceeding by far the best projections of only a few years ago (see figure 1).

The growth of the Church in Latin America is striking enough that a diffusion of knowledge about the Mormon experience there is warranted. This article gives a brief macro review of key historical episodes associated with that expansion, then discusses in depth two key aspects (among four or five worthy of special attention) of the Latin American Mormon experience—nationalism, and authority and leadership. There will be some objections. But we serve both the Spirit and the dignity of our people inadequately if we avoid a discussion of what is on every informed person's mind.

This article is not a commentary on Mormon doctrine, nor is it directed to policymakers. It is not intended for anyone's political arsenal, although some may try to use it for such. The article is intended for students of the Mormon experience in Latin America who seek better to understand the expansion of the Church and to more effectively commit their own lives and fortunes to it.

As indicated in figure 1, the increase in the number of Mormons in Latin America is striking; but more so is the story of the actual propagation of the faith, for herein lies the drama of people's hearts and minds as they struggle with commitment and change, triumph and misfortune.

Figure I.

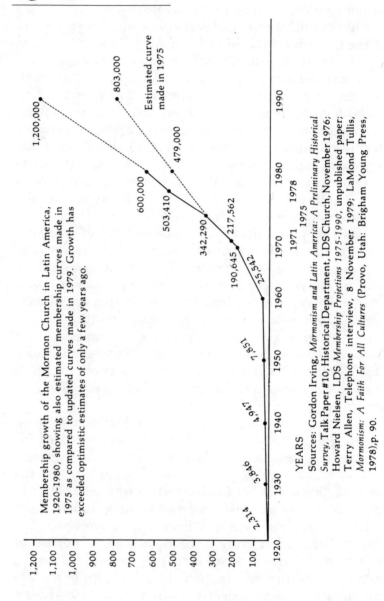

Membership growth of the Mormon Church in Latin America, 1920-1980, showing also estimated membership curves made in 1975 as compared to updated curves made in 1979. Growth has exceeded optimistic estimates of only a few years ago.

YEARS

Sources: Gordon Irving, *Mormonism and Latin America: A Preliminary Historical Survey*, Talk Paper #10, Historical Department, LDS Church, November 1976; Howard Nielsen, LDS *Membership Projections 1975-1990*, unpublished paper; Terry Allen, Telephone interview, 8 November 1979; LaMond Tullis, *Mormonism: A Faith For All Cultures* (Provo, Utah: Brigham Young Press, 1978).p. 90.

The same generation of Mormons so instrumental in the Church from the very beginning, for example, was also the first to take the restored gospel to Latin America. In 1851, only four years after the arrival of the Saints in the Great Salt Lake Valley, Parley P. Pratt, his wife Phoebe Soper, and Rufus Allen set sail for Chile to open the South American mission of the Church. Pratt had long dreamed of such an undertaking and had invested prodigious energies to bring it about. But the first missionary effort in Chile was short-lived, lasting only a few months. A quarter of a century passed before Mormons once again seriously thought about preaching the gospel in Spanish, and nearly three-quarters of a century passed before the Church reopened a mission in the southern half of the Western hemisphere (in 1925 in Buenos Aires, Argentina).

Preparations for cautious exploratory thrusts into Mexico, however, were begun in 1874, with more extensive activities underway by 1879. While five converts were baptized in Hermosillo, Sonora, in 1878, it was in Mexico City and environs that the first branches of the Church were organized. Missionary work continued in central Mexico through 1889.

In the period between 1885 and 1900, Mormonism went to Mexico literally en masse. At that time hundreds of North American Mormons settled in northern Mexico after yet another exodus in pursuit of religious freedom in this instance denied them during the persecutions following passage of antipolygamy laws by Congress. Fleeing U. S. marshals, they hoped for a more tolerant political spirit in a Mexican homeland. For a time they found it. Their settlements grew and flourished.

These English-speaking Mormon colonists in northern Mexico ultimately provided the Church with the expertise it needed to cross the Spanish-language barrier with the gospel message. Having resettled in order to practice their faith in safety and peace, they also found it both convenient and necessary to learn Spanish in order to conduct business and relate generally to the Mexican political and economic environment. Some of the colonists thus learned Spanish; many of their children learned it very well.

In 1901 the colonists again began to send missionaries to the Mexican nationals in whose country they lived. Indeed, in the early years the colonists and their children provided nearly all the leadership and early missionary service for the Church's operations in Mexico. So it was in South America after the mission was reopened there in 1925. Rey L. Pratt, for example, a grandson of Parley P. Pratt and himself a colonies Mormon, was the first Spanish-speaking missionary to return to the South American continent that his grandfather had abandoned three-quarters of a century before. Like Rey Pratt, a long succession of mission presidents and missionaries who have served in Mexico and in Central and South America learned their Spanish in the schools, playgrounds, and orchards of the Mormon colonies in Chihuahua and Sonora, Mexico. The colonies thus proved to be the wedge for the permanent establishment of the gospel in Mexico and, for that matter, in all of Latin America.

When Rey L. Pratt took leave of absence from his position of president of the Mexican Mission in order to accompany Apostle Melvin J. Ballard to South America to reopen the mission there in 1925, he went not to Chile where his grandfather had landed seventy-three years before, but to Argentina. Ironically, it was thought that Pratt's eloquent Spanish-language skills were required more for dealing with government politicians and bureaucrats in Argentina than for preaching the gospel. The actual missionary work was to be pursued among the thousands of German-speaking immigrants, not the Spanish-speaking residents. For this purpose German-speaking Elder Rulon S. Wells was included in the missionary party to facilitate crossing the German language barrier.

With only marginal success among the German

immigrants, however, the missionaries soon turned to other nationalities in Argentina—Italians, Spaniards, and, of course, the old Argentinian stock itself. Many of these were baptized. Thus the national population as well as many immigrant nationalities have contributed strong and faithful members to the Church.

Within ten years after the Ballard-Pratt-Wells party had landed in Argentina, the gospel had also taken root in Brazil. As in Argentina, it had gone first to the Germans, then to many other immigrant nationalities and old-line population stocks. The harvest has been particularly striking in Brazil, a land where the national language, and now also the language of the Church there, is Portuguese.

Latin Americans in Mexico, Central America, and South America have embraced the gospel. So have Latin Americans who live in the United States of America. In the United States live some twelve million people whose ancestral customs, mother tongue, and race are partly rooted to the soil that was once Mexico's and to the heartbeat of Latin-American lands. Mexican-Americans, Chicanos, Hispanos—the names vary; yet whatever they choose to call themselves, they are in some way part of the fourth largest Latin American community in the world, preceded only by Brazil, Argentina, and Mexico. They also have produced generations of Mormons whose strength and fidelity are seen in the records and whose sons and daughters are now represented throughout much of the Church.

Whether in Mexico, Central America, South America, or the United States, the accomplishments of the Latin American Saints have been significant. These accomplishments have, however, not been achieved without problems, misunderstandings, or heartaches. Indeed, now we see that the very magnitude of the Church's contemporary growth increasingly obliges us to take note of the paradoxical sentiments of hope and despair, motivation and frustration, and love and distrust that accompany the expansion of the gospel message today.

The issues associated with these sentiments are as important as they are interesting. We might call them the "enduring issues," because in one form or another they become the subjects of the serious conversation and thinking of many Latin-American and North-American members of the Church. All this is a natural consequence of the efforts of good men and women to recognize and then attempt to solve difficult problems. Thus, just as difficulties arise to occasion despair, frustration, and distrust, so also do Church members seek to resolve the ensuing dilemmas in favor of hope and love. If there are failures—and there are—one should nevertheless not fail to notice the preponderant successes.

If we can talk about the Church from the vantage of both faith and enlightened observation, we may do so as if by scanning the Mormon experience through a telescope and a microscope. From the telescope we view the grand sweep of events that transforms nations and peoples, knowing in advance that the outcome—the triumph of the kingdom—is never in doubt. But if we turn to a microscope and view in magnification smaller parts of the Mormon reality, thereby holding them up for closer inspection. The events of this hour, this day, set the scenarios for magnification—the happiness, the heartache, the dilemma. Only a moment's time at the microscope impresses us that each person's crucial role in the chain of events that links individual lives and feelings with the destiny of the gospel obliges Church members to bring all our faculties of mind and spirit to bear on what is happening to us in these latter days. Sometimes families are won and lost in the Kingdom for odd reasons. Little, if any, of it is predetermined.

In the macro view we find agreement and harmony in Mormonism today: the gospel will prevail—I have no doubt of that; the Lord's plan will not be thwarted; the earth will ultimately be renewed to receive its paradisiacal glory. Yet from the micro view where a close focus may be had on the sentiments and values of individuals and groups—differences of opinion exist about the meaning of what is seen, or even about *what* is seen. Consider two issues in magnification as they relate to Mormons in Latin America—nationalism, and authority and leadership. (Others might have been selected to discuss—schools and education; applying the saving principles and ordinances in Latin-American cultures; literature of the Church in translation; impact of secular laws; missionary activities; evidences of divine intervention; institutionalization of the Church and the growth of stakes; bureaucracy; the building program; temporal and ecclesiastical mobility; gaps between old and new members; cultural activities; status and social class among Mormons; political interface of Church and state; apostate groups; the fall-out phenomenon.)

Nationalism and the Church

Recently as I visited with a stake president in Mexico City, the subject of Arnold Friberg's paintings depicting Book of Mormon characters came up (reproductions of the paintings are bound in some editions of the Book of Mormon). He grew a bit agitated, finally saying: "These paintings are not paintings we can show an educated Mexican. They're all well done, but they show such an enormous ignorance of culture that they are offensive." He referred to them as imperialism in art forms.

His response to this offense was to tell Mexican Latter-day Saint youth to create their own gospel culture, to bring the gospel into every aspect of their lives—music, art, drama, thought, writing. There must be Mexican Saints who write plays and stories with the gospel at their heart. There must be actors, singers, and dancers among the Mexican Saints. Being Mormon makes them different from other Mexicans, he tells them, but being Mexican makes them different from Saints in other lands. They have something unique and valuable to create and share with all Saints and with all Mexicans. With specific reference to the Friberg paintings, he is having Mormon students of art look at Book of Mormon motifs and learn how to be culturally faithful as well as artistically proficient with them. I have seen some of the paintings. The personages do not look like the Anglo-Americans in Friberg's work. They are decidedly Mexican.

Several years ago the speaker at one of Brigham Young University's all-stake firesides declared that "the flag of the United States is the flag of God." One can speculate about the assumptions underlying that statement: America is a land of freedom—the only country in the world that would have permitted the gospel to be restored. From this bosom of freedom and the vitality of its economic system (capable of generating an economic surplus), the expansion of the gospel was made possible. At the same time the Church's heartland was protected, generally, from political raids and the corrupting influence of state bureaucrats.

That is one side. For two weeks following that speech there came through my office a veritable parade of outraged foreign students. The statement about the flag was whispered far and wide and has now become a subject of conversation across the entire face of Latin America wherever Mormons live. So what is the problem? About the "flag of the United States being the flag of God," said a stake president in Latin America, "that was so until about 1865-70. But with President Monroe came the spirit of something else, but certainly not that of God. Nationalism was converted to paternalism, conquest, and imperialism," he concluded.

If the facts are somewhat incorrect as represented by this statement—and they are—the sentiments contained therein are nevertheless widespread among Latin American

Mormons. They remember from their school days, when their own nationalistic sentiments were stimulated heavily, the selection of history their teachers wanted them to remember. They remember James Monroe and the Monroe Doctrine, all right, but only in light of the early twentieth-century "Roosevelt Corollary" to the Doctrine.

While President Monroe had hoped to keep European interests from further intervening in the Western Hemisphere when he announced his Doctrine in 1823, Theodore Roosevelt later asserted that the Doctrine required the United States to prevent intervention by doing the intervening itself. Under his "big stick" policy, the United States sent armed forces into the Dominican Republic in 1905, into Nicaragua in 1912, and into Haiti in 1915. And the United States either directly or indirectly served notice on every other Latin American country that the same could happen to it. So institutionalized became the intervention that American businessmen could hardly hide their disappointment when Woodrow Wilson refused to invoke Roosevelt's corollary on their behalf during the Mexican civil war of 1910-1917 (although Wilson did send troops to Tampico and authorized the Pershing expedition in the north). They were outraged when Franklin D. Roosevelt refused to respond with force to the nationalization of the U. S. oil industry in Mexico in the 1930s.

Those were the exceptions, for by its traditional interventionist philosophy U. S. warplanes piloted by U. S. pilots bombed Guatemala City in 1954; a U. S. equipped and trained invasion force tried to take Cuba in 1961; 22,000 U. S. Marines occupied the Dominican Republic in 1965; and the U. S. has sent military aid to every traditional dictator who ever surfaced in Latin America—Trujillo, Batista, Somoza, Stroessner, and others, all in the name of hemispheric security. In practice, this simply meant giving a few of the elite the means whereby they could continue to suppress the civilian population in their respective countries. Virtually the same intervention process sub-

sequently transpired in favor of the military guardians
who followed the old-style dictators. The Carter administration attempted to change some of these practices, and
to some extent it was successful. President Reagan's
advisors have pressed for a return to old practices.

One sign of a bad policy is its failure. American
intervention in Latin America to prevent changes in the
power structure of a country or to prevent the intervention
of anyone else who might desire to change that power
structure has failed, not because of a grand evil conspiracy—
although there are enough of them around these days—
but because we could not supply enough guns or buy
enough loyalty from enough people to keep an increasingly
mobilized population suppressed forever.

Thus, in the minds of many Latin Americans—many
Mormons included—the Monroe Doctrine's "big stick" has
been followed by exploitive American business, by the
Pentagon, and by the CIA, all of which, they believe, have
combined to corrupt national self-determination and economic development in their respective homelands. From
this perspective, we should be better able to understand a
Latin-American Mormon leader's statement that "if
someone came to my country saying that 'the flag of the
United States is the flag of God,' well, that would be a
virtual scandal here. It would be another indicator of U. S.
imperialism, but of a religious nature." And as another
added, "To speak of the Monroe Doctrine [as it has been
carried out in practice] as God's plan for the Americas is
not only to court divisions within the Church, but to
endanger the lives of missionaries and members in virtually
every country."

Perhaps the magnitude of the unawareness about
these implications is best comprehended by a perusal of a
press release for Latin American newspapers from the
office of a Utah Mormon scheduled to visit Latin America
on behalf of the Church. One entry in his long list of
impressive credentials included former work with the CIA.

"The CIA and the Mormon Battalion will never get you anywhere in Latin America," an influential Latin-American member said. "If it is true that as you write the Church history of this region there are some things better left unsaid, you might start by never suggesting that an influential American member of the Church would ever admit to CIA ties or applaud the Mormon Battalion. The Mormon Battalion offends all of Latin America. Fortunately," he concluded, "the Battalion had no battles. Had it done so the Church would never have been allowed to enter Mexico."

Nationalism—one's loyalty and devotion to his nation, especially in the sense of his having a national consciousness wherein he exalts his own nation above all others and places primary emphasis on promoting its culture and interests as opposed to those of other nations or groups, may be one man's beauty but another's juggernaut. The historical facts of one become the historical lies of another. We select the history we wish to believe; we accept what we desire to know.

For a religion whose boundaries are coterminous with a nation state, all is well. For Mormonism now, however, the "flag of God," the proper expression of art and culture, and a broadened sense of both our destiny and the microcosmic experiences that make it up, will receive diverse expressions in the "multiple Zions"—to use President Harold B. Lee's oft-cited phrase— developing across the face of this planet. Jingoism seems somehow now to be troubling wherever it is practiced in the Kingdom. Forsaking one's sins, political and otherwise, will require making a distinction between the gospel of Jesus Christ and the ideology of nationalism.

A sense of proportion amidst the rapidly escalating events of our time may have been captured by another Latin-American Mormon. "The United States," he said, "should be applauded for its good organization, good methods, advanced and impressive technology, and quality control of production of commercial goods that assure. great satisfaction and worth to humanity. Beyond that, however, the United States should not be particularly applauded." We notice a salient ommission in his statement. This Latin American Mormon has nothing to say about concepts of freedom and constitutionalism that we cherish so much. Perhaps we can understand why by recognizing that the United States has done precious little to foster freedom or constitutionalism in his homeland, and actually has done much to prevent their development. But this brother's sense of balance is captured poignantly when he says, "Errors of the government of the United States are not errors of the Church."

Generally speaking, therefore, the Saints in Latin America separate the Church from U. S. nationalism (although sometimes not their own) and their sentiments about the United States. They believe the Church to be an international church that has a birthright and a homeright as much in their own countries as anywhere else in the world, including the United States. The United States blessed the world with freedom for the restoration of the gospel but, aside from that, Latin Americans do not see the Church as being tied politically to the United States. Latin Americans in general and thousands of Latin-American Mormons tend to love North Americans as individuals. But if nationalistic or jingoistic expressions from the "colossus of the north" surface among them, then America takes bottom position on a ranking of any number of nations (with the possible exception of Spain)— especially in Mexico.

Authority and Leadership and the Church

On the office door of one of my history colleagues is posted the following phrase: "The Past is Prologue—

Study History." I have always objected to the determinism implied in that statement. I have also marvelled that studying history seems somehow not to affect the future much. We have a hard time putting into practice any of the wisdom of the past. Each generation so thoroughly enjoys its own foibles it is reluctant to put them into the context of broad historical meaning.

Not surprisingly, therefore, the authority and leadership parallels of the Church in Latin America, where the faith is now young, and the early Church in Kirtland and Nauvoo, where it was once young, are striking. Now, as then, the institutionalization of leadership well endowed with theory, and praxis in stewardship and consent, patience and long suffering, love unfeigned, and authority righteously exercised takes generations to produce.

Leadership and followership in the Lord's kingdom are inexorably intertwined. When they work well together it is because not only does righteousness prevail, but because the norms of understanding and expectations about leadership and followership are widely shared and accepted. Such an interfacing produces the coding system for communicating authority and eliciting the proper response from followers. That is the ideal, for even Mormons of the fifth and sixth generations have not got it all together, although they have made giant strides since the days of Nauvoo and Kirtland, when the bickering and quarrelling, attacks and counterattacks within the Church created so much havoc.

But consider Latin America. Of approximately 600,000 members of the Church there, over 400,000 were baptized less than ten years ago—nearly half less than five years ago. There are only a handful of second-generation Mormons, and third-and fourth-generation Mormons are rare, usually referring to their ancestral home as one of the small villages around Mexico City from which some members date their Church lines back to the 1880s. There are relatively few priesthood holders with any length of experience. The first high priests—precious few of them—

for the first stake for Latin Americans (Mexico City) emerged as recently as 1961. Now there are over a hundred stakes in Latin America with hundreds of affiliated wards and branches, schools, and seminaries. While growth in leadership capabilities has been truly remarkable, leadership needs continue to border on desperation. Thus we read of stake presidents who are twenty-five years old, bishops and counselors who are twenty-one years old, and bishops appointed to office within three months of their baptism. (Perhaps that is one reason why the active youth in Latin America seem to take the Church so much more seriously than do their active North American counterparts—sometimes weighty responsibilities are placed upon them at an exceedingly tender age.)

Not having had models of Church leadership to observe over several generations, Latin Americans frequently start their leadership experience in the Church from scratch. While it is remarkable to see how fast they mature, and also how many of them exceed the norm of leadership in the United States, it is to be expected that the style of some would be heavily contaminated by the secular culture from which they emerged. Much of this will work itself out in time. (Vigorous attempts are being made to accelerate the timetable through leadership training seminars. The recent upsurge in local missionaries who return home after their missions to serve in local wards and stakes is also beginning to have a positive impact—more so than in the United States because such challenging responsibilities are given the Latin-American youth.)

Yet the exercising of authority in Latin America as it is *traditionally* done, and the exercising of priesthood authority as it *should be* done, are vastly different. Sometimes the consequences are of crisis proportions; sometimes the resulting frustrations are enough to sadden the heart of the most cynical among us.

Authority, the power to determine, adjudicate, or otherwise settle issues, or to have commanding influence over others, has traditionally meant in Latin America the right to control, command, and determine the fate of other people. The rights of control, command, and determination traditionally were not so much attached to laws or general principles as they were to the person of the authority. Hence the phrase so often used in Latin America— "personal authority," or *personalismo*.

Much of the traditional culture of authority is found in contemporary Latin America. In the family and among the sexes, for example, the father or male dominates—a pattern popularly called *machismo*, a condition of extraordinary male self-esteem and self-assertion. Among employees personal authority has been and frequently still is paternalistic, authoritarian, and at times despotic. Among politicians and government bureaucrats, be they elected, appointed, or civil servants, the exercising of personal authority is often excessively self-serving and arbitrary. As such, effective relationships are established by citizens who can most effectively and efficiently massage the personal needs and egos of the individuals in authority. Sometimes this is done with money—what we call bribes— sometimes it is done with brow-scraping deference paying that contains all the pageantry of a medieval world with its lords and serfs.

Latin America has changed in recent years. Large-scale organization associated with economic development has been responsible for much of it. But the nostalgia for and much of the practice of the past somehow live on. In an unguarded moment that nostalgia can and does find expression in the authority relations between some— happily not a majority—stake presidents and bishops and their flocks. Consider the following.

A few years ago, when it was alleged that President Kimball told Church leaders everywhere they were too lenient in dealing with transgressors, a few Latin American stake presidents considered this to be authority to disfellowship and excommunicate members for fairly unconventional reasons. Even minor disagreements of administrative procedure with the stake president became sufficient grounds in some instances for calling a trial to judge one for his membership in the Church.

One young man called to a Church court was disfellowshipped because his bishop reported that he disagreed with the way the sacrament was being passed; another returned missionary was disfellowshipped when his stake president heard he had criticized his conference speech. Another young man was called to court, told there was nothing "against" him, but then was disfellowshipped because he was not humble enough towards his bishop. He appealed. His case went to the high council for a review. All ten high councilors voted to reverse the case, as did also one counselor in the stake presidency. The stake president nevertheless upheld the disfellowshipment, for he had earlier agreed with the bishop to do so—as a *personal* favor. (One high councilor left the Church over this issue.) One stake president even disfellowshipped a member because he would not eat meat. Another set up a plan to excommunicate or disfellowship members who took drugs, controlled or uncontrolled. An elder was excommunicated for failing to sustain a newly appointed bishop when his name was presented in sacrament meeting.

Cultural inclinations reinforced with a private interpretation of President Kimball's alleged counsel have led to some ecclesiastical and leadership atrocities in Latin America. Happily they are not widespread. But where they exist there are, and have been, other implications of a less spectacular but nevertheless troubling nature. One is the retarding of needed leadership development in some stakes. As it is the most prepared and qualified people who tend to speak up against abuses of the kind described above, they find their own membership status placed in question. Either they submit to being cowed or they are driven underground. The Church is thereby, in some places, sometimes not able to enjoy the benefit of its most able people because they are frequently reluctant to get involved. Such behavior turns counselors and advisors into "yes men," for they refuse to voice in private council a disagreement with their leader.

Another implication arises in the handling of individual cases of transgression, or "reported transgression." When a leader excessively contaminated with traditional authority culture— becoming what Latin Americans call a "religious *cacique*"—is personally offended by the sin, he not only comes down hard, but uses the occasion to give expression of his own "personal righteousness." As repentance is not encouraged by conditions that enhance resentment, people leave the Church and return to their sins, transgressions or disagreements. More than identifying and helping people with their problems, the religious *cacique* desires to find a scapegoat and make an example for others to see. This has the same function as "public hangings." None of it encourages respect for authority, although it does sometimes elicit desired behavior.

In most of the Latin American Church there are stake presidents and bishops who are just as long-suffering and considerate of members as one finds anywhere, leaders who seek and who have found the will of the Lord in the exercise of their ecclesiastical and pastoral duties. They inevitably are in conflict with the religious *cacique*, however, and always will be. Alarmingly, there appears to be no way to work the problems out until the *cacique* is released from his position. While there are a lot of casualties along the way, outside observers seem not to get the message. It is highly unlikely that a stake president's decision will be countermanded. If his optimum leadership model is General Patton, as I heard one say, we get a feeling for the struggle yet ahead.

Aside from the general background on the expansion of the Church in Latin America, we have looked at two aspects of the reality of the Mormon experience there that are on the minds of all informed people. Anglo-Americans have been chided on the issue of nationalism, and Latin Americans have been chided on traditional leadership culture. As we look at nationalism, and leadership and authority, through the telescope, Mormons know that in the end the offenses will cease, that members will more closely approximate the Lord's culture rather than their own, and that time-bound concepts of authority, and politics and society, will give way to a greater search for and a more ample willingness to live the Lord's plan for his people. It is that hope that unites Latin-American and North-American members of the Church in an enterprise that will roll forth to consume the whole earth.

But looking through the microscope we have long known that the impact of events on the lives of individuals can be exacerbated or mitigated by individual actions and decisions. We *can* learn from our experience. The past does not have to be prologue.

In the grand scheme what will *our individual* lot be? Kicking hither and yon, demanding molds of character and spirit as parochial as our own minds? Reaching out with the truths of the gospel message in a brotherhood tuned to the galaxy, to the eternities?

While the future will not be painless, Mormons may (as they rise, more experienced and less parochial, to the challenges of the twenty-first century) indeed see a part of the promised brotherhood of Jesus Christ meet its prophetic destiny. Should that be their happy lot, they are certain to rejoice with the heavens in having learned at long last to comprehend the will of the Lord for his people, to comprehend reality and one another, and to understand what may be if they but learn how to help make the prophetic utterances of the centuries come to pass in our very own lifetime.

Notes

1. Specific citations are not given throughout the paper. Quotes from Church leaders in Latin America are from personal conversations with the author and the interviewees should remain anonymous. Other general historical background information is generally known.

2. *Church News*, 29 January 1977, p. 3.

6

Testimony and Technology: A Phase of the Modernization of Mormonism Since 1950

James B. Allen

This paper was orignially presented before the Charles Redd Center for Western Studies on 24 January 1980. The author recognizes that rapid technological development has already outdated some of it.

It seems almost superfluous to mention that we live in a highly technological age. The artifacts are all around us in the form of television sets, telephones, computers, and calculators. In the following essay James B. Allen, Professor of History at Brigham Young University, considers some of the ways in which the technological revolution and the post-industrial age have impacted on the plans and programs of the Church of Jesus Christ of Latter-day Saints.

The effect is broad—perhaps more pervasive than most members realize. Many see general conference sessions on television, but not all are aware of the use of computers and electronic editing equipment in the production of Church publications. Most are aware of the standard plan chapels, but many may not realize that their membership and financial records are stored on computer tape and transferred to hard copy only as needed. Even the temple ceremony and the accompanying genealogical records have felt the impact of this revolution in the temple films and the computerized recording of names and dates.

More important than these adaptations of technology to make the Church programs operate smoothly and effectively is the question of the ultimate impact of technology on Church doctrine and membership

*perception of the nature of the Church. Professor Allen's major theme is
that while practices have changed to meet technological demands, basic
doctrines have not been altered. Professor Allen concludes that though
the impact has been great it has not been detrimental, and he expects that
it will not be in the future. Furthermore, he points to some rather useful
adaptations of new technology such as the more efficient issuing of
missionary calls. He suggests that the Church will adapt to the coming
technological changes with its essential message intact.*

"The British are coming! The British are coming!"
cried Paul Revere, confirming fears long held by the
people, as he rode through the villages west of Boston in
1775. And the villagers heard him, gathered at Lexington
and Concord, and fired the first shots of the War for
Independence.

"The Martians are Coming! The Martians are coming!"
cried terrorized Americans in 1938 as they listened to
Orson Welles's radio dramatization of the "War of the
Worlds." That they should have believed such a story was
incredible, except that somehow their society was becoming
more gradually aware that science and technology had
hardly scratched the surface of the possible, and that
terrible machines capable of wiping out the human race
might someday really exist.

"The computer is coming! The computer is coming!"
cry many fearful Americans today (people whom Alvin
Toffler calls "future haters") as they listen to the prophets
of doom foretell the impending destruction of human
individuality and purpose in the coming technological
society.

In every age there have been people who believed they
had something to fear in the world around them. Sometimes the fear has been rational, other times it has been
irrational, but always it has elicited an active response
when it appeared that the fear was about to become a
reality. The patriots at Lexington and Concord were
justified in their fears of other human beings, and their

rational, well-laid plans were carried out with profound consequences. Americans of 1938 demonstrated a latent fear of some nonhuman force, but they had no plans to confront it when it came, and their response to an unreal situation was irrational. Today some Americans perceive a nonhuman threat, the machine, acting in concert with a human threat, the technocrat, and their response is a campaign to somehow check the stampede of technological innovation before it tramples the race.

So what does all this have to do with Mormon history? Please do not misunderstand. Today's machines pose no threat to the Church, but as the Church adapts new technology to serve its needs, it is worthwhile to approach the subject of Mormonism and technology in the context of the impact of technology on the larger society. The potentialities of technology have probably created more controversy in recent years than any subject other than politics, and many political issues, such as birth control and the environment, are directly related to important scientific and technological developments. If some writers, like Lewis Mumford, compare the technological society to "an automobile without driver, steering wheel, or brakes, but crammed with demoralized passengers hurtling full speed toward doom,"[1] others acclaim it as heralding the golden age of peace, prosperity, and enrichment of the human soul. While we can hardly analyze the Mormon Church in the same terms as the prophets of doom or utopia analyze the larger society, we must nevertheless recognize that the same technological innovations that have so dramatically influenced the world around us have also affected the Church, and that it is not too soon for Mormon historians to begin to assess that impact. We are, in fact, already latecomers to the scene; many popular and scholarly writers have already made their declarations about the impact of technology on the larger society.[2]

I must confess, however, that after spending months attempting to understand the technological advances that have covered only half my lifetime, I was perplexed when it came to writing about them and felt much like Henry Adams as he wrote:

Historians undertake to arrange sequences—called stories, or histories—assuming in silence a relation of cause and effect. These assumptions, hidden in the depths of dusty libraries, have been astounding, but commonly unconscious and childlike; so much so, that if any captious critic were to drag them to light, historians would probably reply, with one voice, that they had never supposed themselves required to know what they were talking about.[3]

But Henry Adams was serious. He had just come from the Great Exposition of 1900, where he stood perplexed before the giant dynamo on display that made him wonder about the changes in society that such a machine forbode. It exuded a potential for physical power that Adams compared with the spiritual power of the Virgin at the Cathedral of Chartres. But he did not understand the new power—he only knew that somehow it was going to make America different, and he was awestruck in its face.

The planet itself seemed less impressive, in its old-fashioned, deliberate, annual or daily revolution, than this huge wheel, revolving within arm's length at some vertiginous speed, and barely murmuring—scarcely humming an audible warning to stand a hair's breadth further for respect of power—while it would not wake the baby lying close against its frame. Before the end, one began to pray to it; inherited instinct taught the natural expression of man before silent and infinite force.[4]

Adams still imputed more power to the Virgin than to the dynamo, but his awe of the new "silent and infinite force" is comparable to the deep respect that many people now hold for the new technology of the past thirty years.

Historically, no one doubts that most of the fundamental changes in the nature of human society have been directly related to scientific discovery and technological innovation. When man reduced his language to visual symbols he made a technological breakthrough that had profound consequences. It not only revolutionized communication, but it created the memory of the race— the means by which each generation could speak to the future. The printing press was another turning point, for it caused a revolution in communications and learning and became the circulatory system of all modern culture, so far as ideas and information were concerned. The modern computer is, in some ways, only an electronic adaptation of these earlier methods of recording language symbols, augmented by sophisticated systems of selective recall and analysis, but it may well have a revolutionary effect upon society comparable to the writing and printing instruments that were among its ancestors.

Religion could not escape the onslaught of science and technology, and in the seventeenth century these forces even required Christianity to create for itself a new heaven and a new earth. When Galileo observed and Newton explained the predictable, unchanging laws that governed the universe, as opposed to the traditional Christian view that everything was in the hands of an arbitrary God, and when technology supported such pure science with the use of the telescope and other marvelous devices, Christianity had to change the way it thought of heaven, of earth, of God, and even of the relationship between God and man.

Providentially, Mormonism did not emerge until after the most wrenching impact of the Enlightenment had been felt, and so its members were not as encumbered with antiscientific tendencies as otherwise they might have been. Since its founding, nevertheless, the world around it has constantly helped mold its history and influence its perspective, and technology has been an important part of that world. The so-called industrial revolution of the nineteenth century, for example, originated with technological innovation, but was "revolutionary" only because it led to fundamental social change and, in the words of

John Diebold, "created a new environment for mankind, a new way of life."[5] By the end of the nineteenth century America had changed from an agrarian, small business economy to an industrialized, urban society dominated by giant corporations and finance capitalism. The effect on the Church was fundamental, though not always well perceived. As the Mormons integrated themselves more fully with the rest of the nation they clearly took on more of the values and perspectives of the business-oriented American society that had been created, in part, by technological innovation. The law of consecration, for example, as instituted by Joseph Smith, was essentially an agrarian system that envisioned a series of small, self-sufficient agricultural communities as the basis of the economy. Though the spirit of "consecration" endured, it would have been impossible for the specific system outlined by Joseph Smith to have survived as the practical economic basis for a multimillion-member church in the urban world of the twentieth century. At least to that degree the industrial revolution affected the economic programs and practical philosophy of the Church.

But the technological revolution had more obvious and, if you will, positive effects on Mormonism as it continued into the twentieth century. The typewriter, the telephone, the radio, the automobile, the movie industry, and countless other developments all enhanced the ability of the Church to administer its organization, improve the lives of the Saints, and promote its interests more effectively in the world.

Then came the aftermath of World War II, when continuing military-related research helped spawn what Daniel Bell and others have called the "post-industrial society."[6] The amount of research, development, innovation, and adaptation that has taken place in the last thirty years literally staggers the mind. One writer observed in 1969 that half the scientific research conducted in the United States since its founding had been accomplished in just the previous eight years, that 90 percent of all the scientists who had ever lived were alive at that moment, and that the amount of money spent on research and development had jumped from $280 million in 1940 to $25 billion nineteen years later.[7] The characteristics of the "post-industrial" society were that it placed more emphasis on producing services than manufactured goods; production was based more on human expertise than on capital; production was automated so that workers functioned as machine monitors rather than machine operators; the new machines were devoted to informational technology, functioning as extensions of the human brain rather than another means of increasing horsepower. But the most awesome aspect of the new age was seen in the linking of computers with automated machinery, such as high-speed printers; with almost every other kind of technological device, such as the telephone; with each other; and even, in some imaginative speculations, with the human mind. Most of us have witnessed this revolution, but the deep change it has already made in our culture has seemed so natural that it was a kind of rude awakening for me as I played backgammon with a home computer and simply could not stop myself from continually referring to my opponent as "him." But I beat "him" two times out of three, so maybe "he" was programmed to calm my fears of the impending computer takeover by making me believe that I was still "his" master.

   Technology, then, is clearly an instrument of cultural change, but what has it done for—or to—the Church in the post-industrial age? Is the Church adapting as readily to whatever new challenges the age presents as it did to those of the industrial era? And what of the future, as technological innovation promises to continue at an even faster pace? I can speak with little or no authority on the last question, but on the first two I think I can provide some provocative insights that may have a bearing on the question of the future.

Like the society around it, the Church has been influenced most profoundly in recent years by computer and communications technology that, when combined with other technologies, has produced results which would have seemed astounding a generation ago. Take, for example, what has happened in the travel industry. In 1952 British Overseas Airways Corporation put the first jet airplane on commercial passenger routes; before long the jet was standard transportation for Church business, and Salt Lake City was less than a day's travel from almost any spot on earth. The advantages to the Church are obvious when one considers the volume of Church business handled by Murdock Travel Agency. Today over thirty-two thousand missionaries a year either leave for or return from missions; some seventy general authorities are constantly on the move throughout the world; and many administrative officers and employees of the Church frequently travel on official Church business. Murdock handles it all, but only with the aid of an Apollo System computer that is keyed in to all major airlines, gives the agency immediate access to flight schedules and seating availability for months ahead, and even orders and prints the tickets.[8] The combination of jet airplane and computer technology saves the Church significant time and money and is also one key to making its worldwide missionary and administrative programs possible.

Advanced publications technology has also become essential to many functions of today's Church. In the last fifteen or twenty years the high-speed web offset press, so named because it feeds and completely prints a continuous web of paper through its several units, has become the backbone of the Church-owned Deseret Press as it attempts to keep up with modern Church demands. The tremendous volume of work includes a million copies of the Book of Mormon in a year and a half, 800,000 family home evening manuals annually, 450,000 Melchizedek Priesthood manuals each year, and the same number of Relief Society lesson manuals. These constitute only a small portion of the work done just for official Church programs, in addition to the millions of volumes produced each year of nonofficial yet Church-oriented publications. In 1977 the Church published its new and updated *Topical Guide to the Scriptures*: a 500-page book containing 640 subject entries and tracings to about 22,000 passages of scripture. Enlisting the aid of a specially designed computer program made it possible for the compilers to complete their four-year job at least ten years earlier than they could have done otherwise.[9]

Perhaps the best known examples of technological innovation in Church programs came in genealogical and temple work. The vast Genealogical Society microfilming program, for example, got underway in 1938 and since World War II has expanded to include well over a million rolls of microfilm stored in the Church's famous granite mountain vault, which contains records from throughout the world. The vault itself, completed in 1963 at a cost of some two million dollars, has the capacity of storing the equivalent of 26 million 300-page volumes—and can be expanded when necessary. The tremendously improved facility for genealogical research and temple work provided just by this innovation is obvious, but beginning in the early 1960s the computer added another dimension. With the goal in mind of keeping the temples supplied with names, the Genealogical Department of the Church supervises a mammoth name extraction program that combines the facility of microfilm with the analytical potential of computer programming. In order to assure accuracy, names and vital data are extracted twice from each roll of microfilm and fed into the computer. The computer makes sure there is enough data to identify the name as a separate individual, checks to see if temple ordinance work has been done (previous temple ordinance data, since 1968, is now on a computer file), and prepares lists for temple work. After the proxy baptism and endowment work has been accomplished, the computer can assist in matching names with each other to identify family group for the purpose of proxy temple sealings. Additionally, paper work has been eliminated almost completely by providing each temple patron with a plastic temple recommend that is inserted into a computer terminal at the time a particular ordinance is to be performed, and the computer takes care of all the recording of data. Equally important: all this is being accomplished with little discomfort to the ordinary temple patron. He still goes to the temple, hardly perceiving the complex electronic data processing that has gone into providing a name for him as he stops at the desk, enjoys the spiritual uplift of the temple ceremonies, and feels satisfied that he is making a significant contribution to the all-important work of salvation for the dead. What's more, technology has made it possible for him to do all this much more rapidly than a generation ago, which provides today's overly busy Saints at least some extra incentive to attend the temple more often.[10]

These are only a few of the more obvious ways that modern technology has been harnessed to enhance Church programs. We could multiply our examples almost without limit, but they include the adaptation of the computer to a multitude of programs (or the adaptation of the programs to the computer, which is a point that will be discussed later); the widespread use of motion picture technology to provide educational films for the Church; public relations; more effective and efficient presentations of the temple ceremony; recording of important historical events; travel; publication and communications technology; and innovations in architecture and building technology—and the list could go on. In none of these areas was the Church in the vanguard of technological development, but it willingly followed the rest of the western world into the post-industrial age by opening its arms to whatever innovation could match its aims.

But there are trade-offs. Almost every technological

decision carries with it some cost, some dissonance, some need for personal philosophical or perceptual adjustments, or some change in traditional programs that have seemed almost sacrosanct to those who have grown up with them. This is the very phenomenon that in the last fifteen or twenty years has given rise to a mass of popular and technical literature raising all sorts of fears about the coming technological society. In 1961 the American historian Perry Miller looked with trepidation upon what he considered the inability of the race to control the machines it was creating, partly because people were simply unaware of technology's potential. He was chiefly concerned with its negative effect, as he saw it, on American cultural and intellectual life, and in an impassioned essay on "The Responsibility of Mind in a Civilization of Machines," he spelled out his fearsome generalizations:

There were, of course, . . . rural backwaters, where the people clung to the simpler economy and there was a certain amount of folk resistance to the temptations of the machine. But on the whole, the story is that the mind of the nation flung itself into the mighty prospect, dreamed for decades of comforts that we now take for granted, and positively lusted for the chance to yield itself to the gratification of technology. The machine has not conquered us in some imperial manner against our will. On the contrary, we have wantonly prostrated ourselves before the engine. Juggernaut seems by contrast an amateur contrivance; we have invented the superhighway, an impressively professional mechanism for mass slaughter.

Miller then commented on the passion with which nineteenth-century Americans "flung themselves into the technological torrent," and added:

We today are still bobbing like corks in the flood, unable to get our heads high enough above the waves to tell whether there are any longer solid banks on either side or whether we have been carried irretrievably into a pitiless sea, there to be swamped and drowned.[11]

As stated earlier, I am not predicting that such dire consequences have resulted, or will result, for the Church as it embraces the technology of the age. But the marriage of technology and religion seems permanent and each new offspring of that union at least raises some important philosophical and cultural questions. The leaders of the Church may well have already considered these questions in their administrative and spiritual context, but the historians will consider them for years to come in their cultural context.

Consider, for example, the modern building program of the Church—certainly an offspring of the union of traditional spiritual concerns and technological innovation. The statistics are impressive, and clearly point up that technology is helping meet the need for economy in handling the sacred tithes of the Saints. In 1979 the Church had some fifteen hundred building projects underway in the United States and Canada, half of which were new buildings and half remodeling projects. Though official totals are not available, it is estimated that the Church begins $1 million worth of new building construction daily and that the ever-increasing annual budget of the building department now exceeds $350 million. All this has resulted in the development of an elaborate program of standard plans, in which costs, new building technologies, efficiency, specialized building materials and, inevitably, the computer all play a role.[12]

Unfortunately, the very idea of standard planning has caused much negative comment from local Church members and leaders, particularly with regard to the architectural sameness of many of the buildings and the perceived difficulty of altering the standard plans to meet local desires. In Orem, Utah, for example, a stake center and a ward chapel are each located on 8th East, just a few blocks apart. Anyone who became a little confused on his exact location could easily get the two buildings mixed, even after going in the front door, because they look so much alike.

In reality, standard planning is not so rigid as some conceive it, and it has much to commend it. The Standard Plans section of the Building Department, formed in 1976, has actually devised about sixty plans, and each of these has two optional forms available, depending upon whether they will be built in warm or cold climates. In addition, there are four more "standard" variables possible for each modified plan, depending upon the earthquake zone involved. This actually makes 480 variations of standard plans available from the Building Department. Some of the variations are minute, of course, and almost imperceptible to the average eye, but the fact that such plans exist is a reflection of a very important concept about Church buildings. These plans embody years of accumulated experience with building use, costs, and a variety of regional differences—and all this accumulated technological know-how is a valuable resource that saves the tithepayers of the Church millions of dollars annually.

In addition, the standard plan program may not be as inflexible as some people think. Today, at least, Building Department managers emphasize the fact that their plans will never fit every local situation, so local architects are hired to adapt the plans to local conditions, methods, and codes. The standard plans, each of which contains twenty-three complete sets of working drawings and specifications, are reproduced in Salt Lake City by a most efficient technological method and then sent to the local architect. His proposed modifications, which may include building material as well as various structural items but not the basic floor plan, are discussed and frequently incorporated into the final product. If some people are dissatisfied with standard plans and try to move heaven and earth to keep from using them, it is significant that there are also local Church officials and Mormon architects who are so convinced that anything sent from Salt Lake City is inspired that they simply will not tamper with it. The

Building Department discourages that attitude, actually seeking some degree of local input. A reasonable combination of the Church's concern for cost, durability, and efficiency with various legitimate local concerns is what the Building Department really seeks.

But what are the trade-offs? The new generation of Church buildings are cost-efficient, durable, adaptable, expandable, reasonably attractive, and relatively easy to maintain. On the other hand, all these advantages are the result of a conscious decision not to allow local architects to create unique designs from "scratch." This is not just a recent development, for there were standard plans as far back as the 1920s. But the hope of producing any building that is a unique or special work of art and innovative architecture, such as some of the nineteenth-century tabernacles and temples, seems largely to have been eliminated by more pressing modern needs. In addition, the interiors of both chapels and modern temples seem sterile by comparison with earlier buildings—not just because they are designed with cost and efficiency in mind, but also because of the prohibitive cost of hiring skilled artisans to produce the decorative columns, murals, stairways, podiums, arched windows and stained glass that once graced so many Mormon buildings. One is reminded of Perry Miller's concern for the mind in the world of modern technology, as we consider the fact that few if any modern buildings will help enhance the Saints' understanding of and appreciation for the best in aesthetic beauty. On the other hand, the very existence of the Church Building Department, with its standard plans, makes at least highly adequate and somewhat attractive houses of worship possible where, under any other system, the Saints simply could not afford them.

Communications technology has raised a series of different kinds of questions, and an interesting article may someday be written on the impact of this technology on one of the Church's most long-standing institutions, the general conference. Conference was first broadcast on KSL television in 1949 and soon went to a national, and even worldwide, audience. This meant using scores of stations that had nothing to do with the Church and yet were willing to broadcast at least one session of conference, either live or by tape delay, as a public service.

The results were most interesting, as the media itself helped mold the institution. There is evidence, for instance, that as conference speakers became aware of the potential number of non-Mormons who could view them, the subject matter of the talks took on more of a missionary flavor, and less preaching directly to the Saints. This was only natural. At the same time, Elder Bruce R. McConkie once reported an analysis of conference addresses in which he believed that the quality of the talks had greatly improved since television, partly because of the much more precise timing and therefore careful written preparation that was needed.[13] The most obvious change was the format of conference, designed specifically to accommodate television stations that must make commercial breaks at certain times. The primary stations, for example, always break at exactly 59 minutes and 27 seconds after the hour and return exactly on the hour, and it is up to Church engineers as well as conference participants to make sure their program conforms exactly to this schedule. In addition, stations must take commercial breaks at intervals between the hour. This has resulted in shorter and more precisely timed addresses, longer and more frequent choir or organ interludes between the addresses, and on occasion the elimination of the closing prayer from the broadcast, since it would be cut off anyway. Naturally there has been much discussion of the role of inspiration in presenting conference addresses, with some Church leaders concerned that such precise timing and exact written preparation would inhibit the flow of inspiration at the pulpit. When Elder LeGrand Richards once good-naturedly raised the question of why they couldn't still let the spirit move them as they got up to talk, President David O. McKay simply replied with equal good nature, "Elder Richards, you let the spirit move you while you're writing the talk."[14]

The result for the Saints, however, has been interpreted generally as more of a blessing than a disadvantage, for at least they have opportunity to participate personally in conference proceedings—right in their own homes. They have learned to live with the interruptions, and even with the sometimes inappropriate commercials that are always aired during the breaks, although the implications of the format have become the subject of some good-natured humor. As one Mormon graduate student wrote while he watched conference not many years ago in his apartment in Lansing, Michigan:

> The Prophet I can plainly see
> At conference time on my TV.
> He stands erect and can be heard
> Right after this "Important Word."

But there is a more substantive concern. We have been awed at the potential audience as conference is beamed from radio and television stations throughout the United States and in other countries, and at the expectation that millions of nonmembers would be tuned in. The reality is that only the members are listening. When Heber Woolsey first went to work as Director of the Public Communications Department of the Church, he commissioned an independent research bureau to conduct a rating on general conference broadcasts. In the Los Angeles area the rating was one—which meant that 99 percent of the TV sets that were turned on that day were not tuned to the Mormon conference. In Washington, D. C., the rating was two; in Phoenix, Arizona, it was seven; and in Chicago it was so low that it did not register.[15] Technology had done much for the Saints, but little for the missionary program. As a result, some new approaches to conference broadcasting are being developed. During the October 1979 conference, on an experimental basis, the Church set up "earth stations" (receiving stations equipped to receive signals from satellites) at stake centers in Atlanta, Boston, Indianapolis, Miami, Philadelphia, St. Louis, Syracuse, Cincinnati, and Dallas. The Church had actually been renting satellite time for all sessions of conference since April 1979, and now the earth stations allowed the stake centers to pick up the broadcast live. If the Church should decide that the missionary potential of its traditional conference broadcasting is nil, and that it wants to direct the conference primarily to Church congregations, the possibilities of satellite transmission are impressive. The 1979 cost of renting satellite time was only $490 an hour— a total cost of less than $4,000 for four sessions of conference, or less than $5,000 if the priesthood session were broadcast. The cost of an earth station, if purchased outright, was about $12,000, although one could also be rented. Would it be worth the cost to equip every stake center in the world (at least so far as government regulations allowed) with an earth station, so that the Saints would gather there and view not just one session of conference, but all of them? (Note that in comparison with the total cost of a building $12,000 is not a very high additional expenditure.) With the relatively low cost of video recorders, a far-away stake could have its own tape delay program to compensate for the time differential. Another important advantage would be the improvement in conference format—particularly the elimination of commercials—once the earth stations were in use and the Church did not have to worry about commercial television stations.

But this is not all—there could be some rather exciting spin-offs so far as internal Church communications are concerned. Suppose the President of the Church wanted to hold a solemn assembly exclusively for the benefit of priesthood leaders in a particular area. He could do it from Salt Lake City via satellite and a now-available coding process. The signal would go to the satellite in code and could be unscrambled only by the decoder on the particular earth station desired. Such technology has almost unlimited possibilities with respect to personal conferences, special messages, training programs, and a multitude of other uses.

The use of communications technology for public relations raises another kind of question. The hardware is there—able to work technological miracles. But what about the "software," or the message itself that the Church attempts to deliver? Are we really using technology to our own best advantage, or have we let the technology use us? This has been a major concern of Heber Woolsey and John Kinnear, Director of the Broadcasting and Films Division. The experience with general conference and with other religious programming suggests that most people simply will not sit down to listen to messages— especially if they are more than thirty seconds long. Is there, then, an alternative way of putting the Church in a favorable light in the minds of large segments of the population through the broadcast media? As John Kinnear and his staff studied the problem, they recognized that television watchers basically wanted entertainment, and if Church programming could not compete with other programming, then there was no use even attempting it.

But this raised fundamental questions. Should the Church go into the entertainment field, just for the sake of publicity? Should it actually buy radio and television time? And should it hire professionals, including non-Mormons, to write and produce its programs? All these questions, if answered affirmatively, would fly in the face of long-held traditions against commercializing the gospel message. One of the most outspoken opponents of buying broadcast time, for instance, was the late Elder Richard L. Evans, who believed the Church should only seek free time, and then give mainly religious or inspirational information. This view continued to be held by many after his death. The problem today, however, as seen by the new public communications experts, is that whatever free time is available is usually the worst possible time, and few, if anyone, would be listening.

But it seems that the new philosophy has prevailed, partly because of the increasing potential of the mass media, partly because of the increasing capacity of the Church to produce excellent "software," and partly because it became clear that the soft-sell approach would really work. Accordingly, the Public Communications Department has instituted a series of programs in the United States especially designed to build a positive image for the Church simply by relating it to something the audience will specifically appreciate and remember. Productions include such things as the well-received "homefront" radio and television public service spots, and the one-hour television show called "The Family and Other Living Things," for which the Church purchased prime time throughout the country. In none of these is there any direct, hard-sell approach—only an effort to provide programming that people will watch because they want to, and to identify it in their minds with the Church.

The "homefront" spots have been especially effective, and the key, according to John Kinnear, is the fact that Public Communications pays special attention to having them written and produced by the best professional talent available—whether or not that talent happens to come from within the Church. Each spot deals with some issue concerning the family, is designed to attract immediate attention, and ends with some statement that identifies it with the Church. In some cases the audience is invited to send for more information, but even in these specially prepared mailers there is no hard sell—only an identification with the Church.

What have been the results? The "homefront" spots are attractively packaged and sent out to all radio and television stations in the country. They range from twenty seconds to two minutes in length, and the evidence is that half of the radio stations and more than 90 percent of the TV stations actually use them at some time or another. Several of the spots have won television's coveted "Clio" award, and in 1979 a two-minute homefront spot called "Try Again" won three Clios—out of twelve hundred entries it was judged best edited, best directed, and the best public service announcement. It is almost unheard of for a two-minute public service announcement to get aired in the first place, and to be listened to for two minutes after that, but the evidence indicates that this one, due to its excellence, attracted the station managers and held the audience.

In the same spirit, the Public Communications Department has gone into other areas, such as the purchase of space for inserts in *Reader's Digest*. The first few inserts were generalized in nature, but they are gradually being moved into specific doctrinal statements, written professionally, and packaged in an appealing format.

Enter, again, the computer. The *Reader's Digest* inserts and many of the radio and TV spots invite reponses, and the number of cards that have come in have mounted into the tens of thousands. As a result, an elaborate computer tracking program is being devised under the direction of Lorry Rytting, Director of Communications Analysis for the Public Communications Department. This program keeps track of who responds, what is mailed to them and when, whether they respond a second or third time, what they respond to, and eventually whether or not they want to see representatives of the Church. It also provides opportunity to analyze the *Reader's Digest* responses in terms of state of origin, comparisons to the *Digest* readership, regional differentials in interest, and the relationship of Church population in a region to reader response. The implications for missionary work are immense.[16]

This leads us, finally, to the whole field of modern data processing, which is the basic function of that most nearly human of all man's machines, the computer. The Church did not approach the computer world quickly or lightly, for the implications were immense, and once any phase of the Church program is in the computer, all other forms of record keeping usually will go by the board. Though "hard copies" of donation records, temple work data, missionary tracking information, and all other sorts of data can be printed out upon demand, the permanent record is only in the computer.

The computer program of the Church grew out of a decision in 1953 to centralize Church accounting procedures in one office and to put the system on punch cards. The first mechanized general accounting ledger went into operation on 1 January 1954, and by 1958 all accounting had been centralized. The punch card system, introduced and supervised by Alfonzo Pia, was the immediate predecessor of the magnetic tape system introduced in 1962 when the first electronic computer was installed in the Financial Department. Gradually other departments began to use it, and in 1968 the Church formed a wholly-owned corporation, Management Systems Corporation (MSC), that provided nearly all the major computing functions for Church programs, as well as a commercial service to other customers. It was recently announced that MSC would be dissolved as a corporation, with the Church portion of its work going directly to the Information Systems Department and the commercial function being sold to a private group. For our purpose, however, I shall continue to refer to MSC, for the transition is not yet (1980) complete.[17]

The importance of the computer to the modern Church is seen in at least two ways: the speed and efficiency with which it can handle data, and the effect it has had on certain traditional concepts and practices. One example is the missionary program. With three to four hundred missionary calls being issued each week, there is an obvious need for computer assistance in the processing. Lest anyone get the wrong idea, however, it should be made clear that the actual decision as to where to call a missionary is still made individually as a select group of general authorities meets each week, considers each missionary recommendation form individually, considers the areas where missionaries are needed, and under inspiration decides where to send them. But the computer makes its contribution in several important ways. It prepares a tally sheet of all the missions in the Church, the number of missionaries in each, and the "complement" for that mission (that is, the optimum number of missionaries desired). It also knows the "lead time" required for a call to each mission, based on such data as the time required to get visas, and other travel concerns, and it can adjust the dating of the call letters accordingly. Eventually the computer will also be able to raise a warning if a particularly complicated call is being considered, such as sending a missionary from one country to another country that does not allow that nationality to come in for the length of time it takes to perform a mission. For example, the Church cannot presently send missionaries from Germany to Australia, and the computer will eventually be able to warn the brethren making the call of that complication. After the call is made, the computer prints out a call letter, with a copy for the bishop, a setting-apart card to go to the stake president, and addressed envelopes. The letters then go to President Kimball's office for his signature. Each month the computer also prepares a roster for each mission that lists chronologically each missionary in the field. A hard copy of the roster is sent to the mission president, who verifies or corrects it and returns it to Salt Lake City. The roster helps the mission president in scheduling releases and transfers, and also helps the missionary office determine where and when new missionaries are needed. When the updated system is in operation the computer will have a direct tie-in with the Apollo computer system at Murdock Travel that will automatically schedule airline reservations and print out tickets. The computer also feeds a computer output microfilm unit (COM) that puts the missionary recommendation forms, together with whatever other pertinent information comes into the office, on microfiche, which is, in turn, attached to a card for storage. Finally, the computer has a tie-in with the minicomputer at the Missionary Training Center in Provo, so that every week it informs the MTC staff of who is coming, when, and so forth.[18]

We have elaborated on this system not only because it is interesting, but also because it contains within it the basic elements of what might be called a practical combination of both spiritual and mechanical necessities in the Church. The sheer bulk of paperwork and human time that would be needed to process all these missionaries, track the needs of all the missions, prepare letters, cards, envelopes, and travel documents, and do all the other routine work would be prohibitively costly for thirty thousand missionaries a year, and would probably result in scores of mistakes. But all of this is merely routine—no inspiration needed except in the matter of the call—and that is the computer's contribution to building the kingdom effectively. At the same time, the Spirit of the Lord can operate as fully as ever—perhaps even more fully—as an apostle, at least two seventies, and the director of pre-missionary services sit down each week to consider each prospective missionary individually. They actually have more information to study out in their minds than ever before, and hence a better data base, if I may be so bold as to apply that term to spiritual things, for the Spirit to draw upon in helping them make decisions. In this respect, then, the computer is not all that awesome in terms of the threat to individual or personal attention.

Other automated systems make equally important contributions to the particular Church program they are involved in. The Automated Donation System, inaugurated in 1970, processes all funds sent to Church headquarters on a weekly, instead of the former monthly, basis, and in the process earns for the Church thousands of dollars per year just in added interest. The high-speed optical reader at MSC accounts for over 20 million contributions per year. The Membership Department has computerized the records of Church members in the United States and Canada, though certain international regulations, particularly with regard to privacy of information, may hinder the extension of that process to some countries. The Church Distribution Centers use the computer for inventory control and to help schedule shipping. The Welfare Department tracks inventories and physical resources. The Payroll Department uses the computer to keep track of and update all its payroll records, as well as print out some 25,000 payroll checks per month. There is even a general authority activity scheduling system that schedules conference visits, makes travel arrangements, and provides other most helpful services. Various departments of the Church, as well as some area administration offices, now have their own minicomputers so that they can put all their necessary records and functions on their own system, without the need to go through the central office in Salt Lake City. These are only some of the many ways the computer program has helped the Church adapt to its growing membership and needs worldwide. In addition, Brigham Young University has its own huge and independent computer program. If one should try to devise a symbol of this mighty technological revolution, it should not be the huge computer itself, but rather the tiny silicon chip that today can perform some twenty thousand computer functions at a cost of one cent per function. By 1990, it is estimated, a chip will contain at least 10 million functions at a cost of less than 1/100 of a cent per function.[19]

How, then, has technology become an agent for change within the Church in the post-industrial era? The answer goes deeper than simply the speeding up of programs and the revolutionizing of data storage and recovery. In some cases it actually strikes at the heart of certain traditions and concepts that some Latter-day Saints have long held sacrosanct.

Consider, for example, genealogical research and the philosophy behind it. Originally it was the teaching of every Church genealogist, and the official policy of the genealogical society, that each person was responsible only for his own family, that temple work could not be performed until names were submitted on verified family group sheets, and that individuals were not to do research on any lines but their own. Throughout the first half of the twentieth century, even when it appeared that some temples might run out of names, Joseph Fielding Smith and others inveighed vehemently against proposals for what they called "indiscriminate name gathering." It was a reflection of a basic change in policy, then, in 1965 when the First Presidency officially informed the Genealogical Society that it had the responsibility of keeping the temples open and that it should initiate a name extraction program in order to do so. Technology did not cause the change in philosophy, but it clearly helped make the change more feasible. As practiced today, it is still the official responsibility for each family to deposit a four-generation family group record at the Genealogical Society and to continue family research, but beyond that Church members are also urged to participate fully in the name extraction program in order to keep the temples running.[20] The change was wrenching to many, but it is only one example of the way technological possibilities have influenced a rethinking of traditional policies and practices.

Other changes are related to temple work itself. Many members remember the time when the motion picture was harnessed to provide the basis for temple instruction, and how many people worried for fear it would not carry the spirit that the live presentations would. The fact is, however, that it was only practice, not doctrine, that was changing, and most people have come to accept the new presentation as well as they did the earlier practice. The computer, however, made something else feasible: the separation of lists for purposes of baptisms, initiatory ordinances, and regular endowments, and then the rematching of the lists and putting them together in family groups for sealings. Some members could hardly fathom the division of the endowment into two parts in the first place, but when it came to keeping the records separately it suddenly appeared that it would be possible for these ordinances to be performed for the dead out of their original sequence—the endowment before the baptism, for example. But the greater value and import seemed to be in getting the work accomplished and having an accurate record made, no matter what sequence the work was performed in. Again, while there was no doctrinal statement as to the order in which ordinances *for the dead* must be performed, traditional wisdom assumed that it must be done the same as for the living. Actually, the temples still get the ordinances done in the traditional order, but the 1965 policy decision as supported through computer programming made it *possible* for that sequence to be upset, and the leaders of the Church did not seem to be inspired to insist upon a traditional practice just for the sake of tradition itself.[21]

Has the Mormon Church been a "leader" in the adaptation of technology? For the most part the answer seems to be no. Certainly the Church had nothing to do with the development of most of these technologies as such, though in some cases, such as the microfilm program, it has gained a worldwide reputation for the breadth of its work. But the kinds of programs it has adopted, except for genealogy, are little different in kind from many others. The Church may have over two million names on its automated membership rolls, but the U. S. Social Security Service has 200 million and the U. S. Army has 80 million. Church accounting files are no more complex or extensive than many others throughout the world, and its total use of microfilm is very small compared with other programs. According to one expert, for example, the federal Social Security Administration uses more microfilm in a day than the Church does in a year. The Church is neither the biggest nor the best in any of its adaptations of technology. But that, after all, is insignificant so far as the real meaning of technology in the Church is concerned. What really matters is whether the Church has been able to adapt its traditional ways of doing things when technology opened doors to better ways of achieving its ultimate spiritual goals, and whether the Church could recognize what effect the modern world was having on it. Only the historians of a few generations from now will be able to answer all these questions with much perspective, but at the moment there is little reason not to view the answers optimistically.

How do Mormons generally perceive technology? Do they see it, as many authors do, as a kind of tool of the devil, as a neutral force, or as the evidence of the hand of God in helping the Church perform its mission? No fully adequate survey has been taken, but Professor Todd Britsch of BYU, along with a few colleagues, has taken some interesting preliminary surveys among Mormons, Catholics, and Protestants in Utah. In general the results suggest what one might expect based on the cultural backgrounds of the people involved. Twelve technological advances were listed, and respondents were asked to rate each as good or bad on a scale of A to E. Birth control pills and mind drugs were rated generally bad by Mormons, artificial insemination was split between good and bad, with a slight edge on the positive side, and everything else was rated generally good. This included nuclear power plants, insecticides, televisions, automation, computers, biological weapons, supersonic aircraft, space exploration, and alternate power sources.[22] One suspects that these Mormons, following some of their leaders, could discern the hand of God in many of these developments—perhaps seeing in modern technology a fulfillment of Orson Pratt's prophecy uttered in 1878:

There must be something connected with the sound of this first trump [opening the millennium] that is miraculous in order that all nations may hear it. . . . There will be something connected with the sounding of the trump of the first of the seven angels which will manifest a power which we know nothing of. The sound of that trump will be heard by all people, nations, kindreds, and tongues in the four corners of the globe. I do not know that the sound will be so much louder than some we have heard, but it will be carried by some miraculous power so that all people will hear it.[23]

Nearly a century later President Spencer W. Kimball commented on the wonders of modern communications technology—radio, television, satellites, portable cassette tape players—and added,

With the Lord providing these miracles of communications, and with the increased efforts and devotion of our missionaries and all of us . . . surely the divine injunction will come to pass: "For verily, the sound must go forth from this place into all the world, and unto the uttermost parts of the earth—the gospel must be preached unto every creature."[24]

The day of the miracle, then, is upon us. But what can we say of the future and of the potential impact of technology on values? For example, how will we avoid becoming so enamored of the machines themselves and the data they spew forth that we lose the sense of dealing with individual people with their many differing needs and perceptions? Can a conscious program be devised to make doubly sure that the fears thus popularized by science fiction have no place within the Church?

This leads to the question of how technology will affect Church planning. In the larger society technology has had an important impact on planning and management development in both business and government—and the theory upon which such planning and development is based. Within the Church the planning of various departments has been influenced by whatever technological innovations seemed useful at the time, and the Information Systems Department coordinates the planning and use of computer facilities. Yet, there is no apparent effort to develop a systematic theory of technological planning or management for the Church as a whole, or even to devise long-range projections concerning the coordinated development and use of multiple technologies. The Church as an institution seems to be content to look conservatively at whatever is happening, then to adapt slowly to technlogical innovation as it becomes beneficial. Little thought seems to have been given to how some goals may change because of technology. Would such planning be beneficial?

Is technology actually contributing to a decline in appreciation for the skills of the dedicated artist and artisan? If so, what can be done to bring about a renaissance of appreciation among the Saints for everything that is "virtuous, lovely, of good report or praiseworthy?" Or, will values change, so that technology itself helps determine what is beautiful or praiseworthy?

Will the current craze for entertainment and easy education result in the creation of some kind of gospel computer game that will go even further than the gospel board games and gospel card games that glut the Mormon market? Could such a development encourage the creation of a generation that glories in memorizing facts and scriptures without the challenge to obtain the deep spiritual understanding that can come only by contemplation rather than memorization and score-counting? When the game of computer salvation finally arrives, in whatever form, can it be used to encourage rather than discourage truly thoughtful study of the scriptures and all other good books?

What will be the Church's response if science and technology make discoveries that challenge fundamental views toward life, man, and the relationship of man to the universe? For example, if science succeeds in creating a successful human clone, what will be the effect on Church doctrine? What if science succeeds in modifying the genetic code to the extent that it can change the forms of future generations of mankind? Is Mormon doctrine so rigidly defined that it cannot adapt to such changes if they come, or are there still areas where current perceptions are not so unbendingly defined that it would be impossible to reconsider and refine them as more knowledge from the world outside the Church impinges upon it?

Mario Bunge in his essay on the "Philosophical Inputs and Outputs of Technology," makes some interesting observations in this regard. After a discussion of the metaphysics, values, and ethics involved in technology, he comments on the "Dubious Morals of Technology." Some ways of knowing, he says, may be morally objectionable, even though knowing is a good in itself. Torturing or killing people in order to find out more about the nature of fear, for example, is morally wrong. But in technology (as distinguished from pure science) some ways of knowing may be suspect, and the entire technological process may be morally objectionable for aiming at evil goals. For example, Bunge calls it wicked to conduct research into forest defoliation, poisoning of water reservoirs, maiming of civilians, and manipulation of consumers or voters, because the knowledge gained in such research is likely to be used for evil purposes.

It is only very recently that most of us have come to realize that technology itself can in fact be wicked and must therefore be checked. We have learned that, while accelerating advance in some respects (such as the size of the GNP), technology is also accelerating our decline in other respects (such as the quality of life) and is even jeopardizing the very existence of the biosphere.

Of course, there is nothing unavoidable about the evils of technology. Except for isolated cases of unexpected bad side

effects, technology could be all good instead of being half-
saintly and half-devilish. It is up to the policy makers to have
the technological investigator produce good or evil
technological items. It is up to the technologist to take orders
or to disobey them. In any event, technology is not by its
nature morally committed one way or another, and its needs
some ethical bridling.[25]

The implication of all this for Mormons is simply the
question of whether those who discuss or define doctrine
will brand certain technologies as evil—because they have
the potential of hurting the Church or the Saints. Or, will
they simply caution the Saints not to bend too readily with
every new challenge to faith and morals, for the Church
has never defined certain "mysteries" with inflexibility?
Or, is some other approach more appropriate?

It is, of course, impossible to answer all these futuristic
questions. It would not be too far reaching, however, to
venture one general prediction: the future will see technological advances we can hardly dream of today, and the
Church, if it holds true to form, will only slowly adapt. But
it *will* adapt, especially if the developments are perceived as
aiding in its goal of taking the gospel to all the world as well
as in its practical need simply to govern the ever-growing
kingdom. Such advances will not necessarily result in a
decline in spirituality, though they may require some
fundamental reconsideration of traditional religious inter-
pretations and viewpoints. And the Church will survive
whatever will come, as it has in the past, and go on in the
post-industrial society as a viable force for good. Continuing technological progress, perhaps kept within limits
by whatever "ethical bridling" the Church can bring to
bear upon it, can in the main be expected to be a positive
force.

Notes

The author expresses special appreciation for the research assistance of J. Michael Allen, Martha Bradley, Jessie L. Embry, and Kimberly Jensen James, as well as the Charles Redd Center for Western Studies and The James Moyle Oral History Program at the Historical Department of the Church of Jesus Christ of Latter-day Saints.

1. As paraphrased in Alan Temko, "Which Guide to the Promised Land: Fuller or Mumford?" *Horizon* 10 (Summer 1968): 28.

2. The literature reflecting the impact of technology on both life and thought is abundant. An excellent starting place is Thomas Parke Hughes, ed., *Changing Attitudes Toward American Technology* (New York: Harper & Row, 1975), which contains twenty-four well-chosen essays. The footnotes at the end of Hughes' introductory essay provide an excellent guide to further reading. A few of the more interesting books consulted in the preparation of this essay included: Isaac Asimov, *Science Past—Science Future* (Garden City: Doubleday, 1975); George Bugliarello and Dean B. Doner, eds., *The History of Philosophy and Technology* (Urbana: University of Illinois Press, 1973); D. S. L. Cardwell, *Technology, Science and History* (London: Heinemann, 1972); Arthur C. Clarke, *Profiles of the Future* (London: Victor Gollancz Ltd., 1974); John Diebold, *Man and the Computer: Technology as an Agent of Social Change* (New York: Praeger, 1969); Victor Ferkiss, *The Future of Technological Civilization* (New York: George Braziller, 1974); Bernard Gendron, *Technology and the Human Condition* (New York: St. Martin's Press, 1977); C. C. Gotlieb and A. Borodin, *Social Issues in Computing* (New York: Academic Press, 1973); Herbert J. Muller, *The Children of Frankenstein* (Bloomington: Indiana University Press, 1970); James Martin and Adrian R. D. Norman, *The Computerized Society* (Englewood Cliffs, N. J.: Prentice-Hall, 1970); Lewis Mumford, *The Myth of the Machine: The Pentagon of Power* (New York: Harcourt Brace

Jovanovich, 1970); Ben B. Seligman, *Most Notorious Victory, Man in an Age of Automation* (New York: The Free Press, 1966); Edward Semper et al., eds., *Hidden Factors in Technological Change* (Oxford: Pergamon Press, 1976); Manfred Stanley, *The Technological Conscience. Survival and Dignity in an Age of Expertise* (New York: The Free Press, 1978); Alvin Toffler, *Future Shock* (New York: Random House, 1970).

3. Henry Adams, "The Dynamo and the Virgin (1900)," a selection from *The Education of Henry Adams,* as quoted in Hughes, *Changing Attitudes Toward American Technology,* pp. 170-71.

4. Ibid., p. 169.

5. Diebold, *Man and the Computer,* p. 3.

6. See chapter 3 of Gendron, *Technology and the Human Condition,* and especially footnote 7.

7. Diebold, *Man and the Computer,* pp. 7-8.

8. Research notes prepared by Martha Bradley, after conducting interviews at Murdock Travel, October 1979.

9. *Church News,* 1 October 1977.

10. My forthcoming manuscript on the history of the Genealogical Society of the LDS Church will have a major section dealing with technology and genealogical work.

11. Reprinted in Hughes, *Changing Attitudes Toward American Technology,* pp. 68-69, from *The American Scholar* 31 (Winter 1961-62).

12. See "Building at $1 Million a Day Pace," in *Building Design and Construction* (December 1979), pp. 104-09. This article is based on interviews with officials of the Church Building Department, and is very responsibly done. Information here comes from that article as well as from interviews by Martha Bradley with Robert Little, Director of Standard Plans in the Church Building Department of the Church of Jesus Christ of Latter-day Saints, and Duane Bracken, draftsman in Standard

Plans, November 1979. See also Martha Sonntag Bradley, "The Church and Colonel Saunders': Mormon Standard Plan Architecture," (Master's thesis, Brigham Young University, 1981).

13. John Kinnear, Oral History, interviewed by James B. Allen, 1979, typescript, the James Moyle Oral History Program, LDS Church Archives, Salt Lake City, Utah.

14. Ibid.

15. Heber G. Wolsey, Oral History, interviewed by J. Michael Allen, 1979, typescript, pp. 24-25, the James Moyle Oral History Program. See also John Kinnear Oral History.

16. Lorry E. Rytting, Oral History, interviewed by James B. Allen, 1979, The James Moyle Oral History Program.

17. Important information and insights concerning computers and their use in the Church were obtained for this paper during a tour of the facilities of Management Systems Corporation, 9 November 1979, escorted by Woodroff Jones, Account Representative; Golden A. Buchmiller, "Computers Aid the Church," *Church News*, 2 June 1979; and the following typescript interviews that are in the collection of the James Moyle Oral History Program, LDS Church Archives: Gary Carlson, Director of Computer Services, Brigham Young University, interviewed by James B. Allen, 1979; Lyle J. Gardner, Managing Director of Data Administration Support for Information Systems Department of the Church, interviewed by James B. Allen, 1979; Royden Olsen, Assistant Director of Translations Services Institute, Brigham Young University, interviewed by J. Michael Allen, 1979; Alfonso B. Pia, Treasurer, Management Systems Corporation, interviewed by James B. Allen, 1979.

18. Interview with Robert Swensen, Director of Pre-Missionary Services, Missionary Department of the LDS Church, by James B. Allen, 7 January 1980.

19. Estimates such as this are quickly outdated, never really accurate, and are used only to dramatize the potentialities. This estimate is drawn from a *proposed* script for a filmstrip by the Information Systems Department of the Church.

20. This change is traced in my forthcoming manuscript on the history of the Genealogical Department of the Church. It should be noted that members are not told that the four generation program is the end of their family responsibilities—only that it is a prime requirement. They are to search out their families as far as possible, but also participate in the name extraction program. Elder A. Theodore Tuttle of the First Council of the Seventy, for example, emphasized both in his April 1980 general conference address. See his address, "Eternal Links that Bind," in the *Ensign*, May 1980, pp. 40-41

21. See Carlson Oral History, passim, for various comments on this.

22. Information obtained from Professor Todd Britsch. The research is still ongoing, and therefore is not available for general distribution.

23. *Journal of Discourses*, 16:327-28.

24. Editorial in the *Ensign*, October 1975, p. 11.

25. Mario Bunge, "Philosophical Inputs and Outputs of Technology," in Bugliarello and Doner, *The History and Philosophy of Technology*, pp. 276-77.